A STUDENT'S GUIDE TO LAW SCHOOL

Chicago Guides to Academic Life

A Student's Guide to Law School

WHAT COUNTS, WHAT HELPS, AND WHAT MATTERS

Andrew B. Ayers

The University of Chicago Press   Chicago and London

Andrew B. Ayers is an appellate lawyer in Albany,
New York.

The University of Chicago Press, Chicago 60637
The University of Chicago Press, Ltd., London
© 2013 by The University of Chicago
All rights reserved. Published 2013.
Printed in the United States of America

22 21 20 19 18 17 16 15 14 13   1 2 3 4 5

ISBN-13: 978-0-226-06722-3 (cloth)
ISBN-13: 978-0-226-06705-6 (paper)
ISBN-13: 978-0-226-06719-3 (e-book)
DOI: 10.7208/chicago/9780226067193.001.0001

Library of Congress Cataloging-in-Publication Data

Ayers, Andrew B.
    A student's guide to law school: what counts,
what helps, and what matters / Andrew B. Ayers.
            pages. cm. — (Chicago guides to academic
life)
    Includes bibliographical references and index.
    ISBN 978-0-226-06722-3 (cloth : alk. paper) —
ISBN 978-0-226-06705-6 (pbk. : alk. paper) —
ISBN 978-0-226-06719-3 (e-book) 1. Law—Study
and teaching—United States. I. Title II. Series:
Chicago guides to academic life.
    KF283.A947 2013
    340.071'173—dc23

                                2013005899

⊚ This paper meets the requirements of ANSI/NISO
Z39.48-1992 (Permanence of Paper).

*To my sister Liz, who once told me she
was thinking about law school.*

Just in case.

The torch of chaos and doubt—
this is what the sage steers by.

CONTENTS

Introduction

In May 2006, a seven-year-old boy named Braxton Bilbrey became the youngest person ever to swim from Alcatraz Island to San Francisco. When he got to the shore, there were some reporters waiting. One asked him what the hardest part was.

He said, "The swimming."[1]

In the beginning, law school feels like that. Everything feels like the hardest part, because you don't see things clearly yet. You don't know what's important and what isn't. You can't tell which parts of the reading to focus on and which to skim. You don't know what to write down in your notes. I would have spent a lot more time panicking in my first year, except that I didn't yet know which parts of law school I was supposed to panic *about*.

I wasn't alone. According to one study, "the emotional distress of law students appears to significantly exceed that of medical students and at times to approach that of psychiatric populations."[2] Everybody feels lost in the first year of law school. If you don't, you're probably not paying close enough attention.

One of the best cures for stress is a sense of control. But you can't take control until you understand what's happening to you. So this book will help you understand the daily choices you make in law school, and how they affect your grades and your future.

Law school requires you to make a lot of decisions. You'll decide what to focus on when you do your nightly reading, what to put into your notes, whether to raise your hand in class (and if you do, what to say), whether to join a study group, how long to spend on each exam question, and so on.

This book will help you see those choices clearly. You'll make the choices yourself.

You'll make better choices if you know what your goals are. I'm going to assume you have two goals: to get good grades in law school, and to become a good lawyer. Here are the two most important things you need to know about how to accomplish those goals:

First: The secret to getting good grades is to treat all of your course work as preparation for the exam.

Second: Good grades alone won't make you a good lawyer.

The rest of this book will explore these two ideas. Parts 1, 2, and 3 will explain how focusing your work on the exam can make your grades better. Part 4 will explain how other choices you make in law school affect the kind of lawyer you become.

This book is an operating manual, designed to guide you through the choices a law student faces every day. I wrote the core of this book immediately after I finished law school, because I didn't want to forget how those choices looked to someone actually facing them. It's one thing to hear from the scientist about what route the rat took through the maze; it's another thing to hear from the rat how he solved it.

I'm going to assume that you are an intelligent adult; I won't tell you to pay attention in class or remind you how important it is to work hard. It's not that paying attention and working hard are unimportant. They're very important. In fact, the secret to doing well in upper-level classes might be working as hard as you worked your first year. One study found that third-year law students spend half as much time studying as first-year students. The median third-year student spent about as many hours studying as a first-year student in the fifth percentile.[3] So if you keep working at the same level throughout law school, you might rocket to the top of your class by default.

But that's about all the advice I'll give you on hard work. I trust that you can figure out for yourself how hard to work, and how often to go to class, and how often to exercise, and whether to go to the bathroom during exams. (All of these questions are discussed in some detail in other law school books I've read—even the one about going to the bathroom.) I want to help you understand the structure of how law school works; this is not a lifestyle guide.

How to Get Better Grades

In most law school classes, your entire grade is determined by one exam. To do well, you'll have to think of all your course work in terms of how it will help you on the exam. Working efficiently toward the exam will help you make better use of your hours in the library; it will help you see the law more clearly; and it will help you free up time to relax. The first three parts of this book will help you understand how it works.

The book begins by explaining how law school devises your grades— which means exams. Part 1 explains how exams work and what kind of preparation is required to do well on them. Rather than telling you what to do, I emphasize the choices you'll make. There's no single right way to take an exam. But there are specific choices every student faces. It's important to think them through.

Part 2 explains the skills that are required to do well on exams. "Thinking like a lawyer" consists of three closely related skills: *distilling* the legal materials you read; *spotting the issues* that your exams expect you to address; and *making arguments* about those issues using the law you've distilled. These are the skills that will determine how well you do on exams.

Part 3 explains how your work during the semester can prepare you for exams and develop the skills they test. It explains how to treat each of the different kinds of work you do in law school—reading, listening to class, and so on—as exam preparation. I'll try to show you how to focus each of these kinds of work on the exams: to strip away the things that won't help you on exams and spend the most possible time on the things that will. This is the part of the book that will interest you most if you're now a first-year student, because it's full of tricks and specific suggestions. Why not put these at the beginning of the book? Because I don't want you to just mimic my study habits; I want you to develop your own. To do that, you'll need to understand what law school wants from you, and what makes some approaches better than others. Parts 1 and 2 give you a foundation for that.

The Costs of Ruthless Efficiency

Doing well in law school means more than getting good grades. The purpose of law school is to make you a lawyer, not just a law school exam taker. If law school teaches you nothing more than how to prepare for an exam with ruthless efficiency, you will have wasted years of your life and vast sums of money. What *else* you'll try to learn in law school depends on your law school, your professors, and your own goals. But every good legal education offers you more than just the bits of law you'll use on exams. Ruthless efficiency can make you miss some of the most important parts of your education.

Law isn't just a collection of doctrines; it's a culture. To do law well you must become, as one professor writes, a connoisseur.[4] Becoming a good lawyer requires more than an intellectual understanding of rules. You'll need a feeling for how the whole system of legal ideas fits together, and how it affects the people who work with it. That's why you go to class: to develop a feeling for how good lawyers talk, argue, and interact.

Your extracurricular life matters too, not just to your sanity but to your prospects of getting good at lawyering. Some of the most valuable parts of law school are extracurricular, like the pro bono work you get to do and the chats with your professors and colleagues that go beyond what's covered in class. All of these things develop your feeling for the law. And all of them take time away from exam preparation. It's important to accept that. In law school, it often seemed as though my mental filing cabinet had only two drawers: one marked *Retained for Use On Exam* and one marked *Banished from My Thoughts*. You'll need more drawers.

The pressure of the exam will tempt you to cut uncredited learning experiences out of your life. You'll feel pressured to skip anything that isn't directly related to getting good grades. It's a difficult balance: on the one hand, exams are always looming, demanding all your time and energy. On the other hand, a good law school offers you a rich variety of intellectual and practical experiences that won't show up on your transcript. No book can make these choices easy for you.

Nor can any book tell you how to balance the pressure of impending exams against all the other things that sensible people want to get out of their lives: friendship, love, music, television. Your choices about how to integrate your work and your life will be a central part of your new identity as a law student, and as a lawyer. A book like this can only help you see those choices clearly, and understand what's at stake.

One of the biggest choices law students make, of course, is the decision to go to law school in the first place. There's an ongoing debate and a fast-growing literature on the value of law school—on whether law school is worth the heavy debt burden many students take on, whether lawyers' job prospects are good enough to justify the financial risks involved, and whether law schools do enough to help prospective students understand those burdens and risks. It's important to know, before you get started, that while some lawyers think going to law school was the best decision they ever made, others deeply regret it. If you're still deciding whether to go law school, I encourage you to research these questions thoroughly, and to reflect on why you want to go to law school and what you hope to get out of it.[5] This book aims to show you how law school *can* be a wonderful experience; please don't mistake that for a promise that it *will* be a wonderful experience. It's a book about how to make the most of law school, not whether to go.

This book also won't try to tell you what law school will feel like. If you want descriptions of the archetypal first-year experience, read Scott Turow's memoir *One-L*, or watch the movie *The Paper Chase*—you'll be relieved when you get to class and it's nothing like the picture they paint. The archetypal law school experience isn't terribly relevant to your experience. There are too many different law schools, too many different professors. And even among the students in a single class, every student's experience is different.

Consider how many different ideas about law school there are, for example, among the many illustrious professors and legal thinkers who've written about it. Duncan Kennedy sees in law school a deadening perpetuation of unjust social hierarchies, a trap.[6] On the other hand, Martha Nussbaum sees in it the potential for a truly Socratic education—one that teaches students not just to analyze law but to find meaning in their own lives.[7] Gary Bellow called law school "empirically irrelevant, theoretically flawed, pedagogically dysfunctional, and expensive."[8] But Oliver Wendell Holmes said that it can show you "the joy of life become an end in itself."[9]

Each of these pictures of law school is real to some law students. Law school is a trap, *and* a soul transformation, *and* a scam, *and* a joy. Your own experience will be determined partly by your professors, your law school, and your peers. But much of it will be determined by your own choices. The more you understand the structure of what's happening, the better the choices you'll be able to make.

Most books about law school warn you, excitedly and often, that law school is completely different than anything you've ever done before. Sure it is, in some ways—certainly in volume, and no doubt in style. But it's learning; you've learned before. You can do this. Especially if someone helps you understand how it works.

> Studies have shown that the best way to learn is to have frequent exams on small amounts of material and to receive lots of feedback from the teacher. Consequently, law school does none of this.
>
> JAMES D. GORDON III, *The Yale Law Journal*, 1991

PART I

The Way You're Judged

Law school exams are what measure your work in law school. In most classes, your entire grade is based on a single exam at the end of the semester. Some professors give you points for class participation, but that's generally a tiny part of your grade. In most classes, the exam *is* your grade.

So before we talk about how to take notes or participate in class, we need to talk about the exam. It may seem strange to find the chapters on exams before the chapters on reading, classes, and note taking. But as you do your reading and your note taking, you'll have to make hard decisions: What should you focus on? Where should you spend your energy? You can't answer those questions without understanding the exam.

Before we start, let's acknowledge the widely held view that law school exam practices are, as one study concluded, an "abomination."[1] Evaluating students on the basis of a single exam at the end of the semester, the authors of that study wrote, "is neither valid, reliable, nor fair."[2] A former president of the American Bar Association wrote, "Is there any educational theorist who would endorse a program that has students take a class for a full semester or a full year and get a single examination at the end? People who conduct that kind of educational program are not trying to educate."[3]

Ideally, the purpose of an exam isn't just to rank students; it's to help them progress in their thinking. But an exam can't play this role very effectively if it comes at the end of the course. Also, an ideal exam asks for thinking that resembles the thinking that's been done in class. This isn't just a matter of fairness; it's a matter of accuracy—the exam doesn't measure performance if it tests something you haven't been learning. But in many law school classes, the exam doesn't much resemble the semester's work.

Still, law school exams aren't totally arbitrary. The skills you need on exams can be developed during the semester, if you make good use of your time and opportunities. The more you understand the skills you'll need for exams, the more you'll be able to develop those skills during the semester.

A word of warning: parts 1, 2, and 3 of this book are devoted, mostly, to showing you how to do well on exams. It would be easy to read these chapters as implying that exams and grades are what matter most in law school. This is a message that law school itself sometimes reinforces; during the first year, some law students begin to think that grades are the most important measure of their worth as a lawyer.

But grades aren't the only thing that matters. As the book moves along, I'll try to help you learn to recognize the parts of law school that matter just as much as exams. Part 4 of the book tries to show you some of the things that matter: other skills, and other kinds of preparation for lawyering. And part 2 points out some of the other things that can be overlooked when students focus too rigorously on exam preparation: other intellectual benefits, and even pleasures, that law school has to offer. But exams do matter. They're the way law school measures you, so you need to understand them.

[E]xaminations and toilets are the only places in our society where puking is permitted.

PAUL N. SAVOY, *The Yale Law Journal*, 1970

1 What Exams Want

Most law school exams are stories: long, complicated sets of facts in which cars crash, businesspeople break promises, police act thuggishly, and unpleasant things are done to people with questionable pasts. At the end of the story, the exam will ask something like, "Who can sue whom?" Your job is to go through the facts and make sense of it all.

Read this unrealistically short example of an exam question, and consider what skills you'd need to answer it. It deals with torts, one of the core subject areas taught in the first year of law school. (For now, you can think of "torts" as "things you can sue someone for, other than breaches of contract.")

A sadistic law school professor gives an exam that's absurdly difficult. Nobody knows any of the answers. One of the students has an unusual anxiety disorder, and has a heart attack, which she barely survives. Another, losing his mind temporarily, attacks one of the proctors, a woman named Proctor, breaking her arm.

The professor, it turns out, got the exam from a website that encourages professors to work out their aggression by giving impossible exams. The website is run by the members of a religion called Belligerism, which encourages its followers to start conflict wherever possible.

Needless to say, several lawsuits follow. Explain who sues whom, and why, and who wins.

Your answer will discuss each of the various legal issues raised by this fact pattern. The exam won't tell you what those issues are; it's your job to identify the legal questions you'll be answering. For each legal issue—each question—you'll then discuss the best arguments on both sides.

Traditional Exams Require Three Skills

Exams are typically graded using a point system. Professors give you points for specific things they like in your answers. You get points for three different kinds of things, each of which requires a different skill:

(1) Identifying the relevant legal concepts. This requires the skill of *distilling the law*: turning the long, difficult legal texts you read into concise, well-articulated statements of the legal principles they contain.
(2) Identifying the legal questions that the exam's fact pattern raises. This requires the skill of *issue spotting.*
(3) Identifying the best legal analysis that supports either answer to a given legal question. This requires the skill of *argument.*

Those three skills—distilling, issue spotting, and argument—are the three skills you'll need in traditional law school classes. Part 2 of this book talks about each of them in detail. This chapter gives you a quick overview of how you'll deploy these skills on exams.

Distilling the Legal Propositions

To do well on exams, you have to have the relevant legal doctrines at your fingertips. You can't spot legal issues or make legal arguments unless you understand the issues you're looking for and arguing about. So you'll need to have distilled the law over the course of the semester. Distilling means creating succinct, well-articulated statements of legal principle that summarize the complicated, jargon-filled legal texts you read during the semester. In other words, it means reducing your reading to *legal propositions*. A legal proposition is a single concept, like "no one under thirty-five can be president" or "the purpose of a legal system is to resolve conflicts peacefully." You will spend a great deal of time during the semester trying to reduce your reading to brief, useful statements like these, because at exam time they're indispensable.

On a typical exam, you'll get some points just for correctly identifying the legal doctrines that are relevant to the problem. You won't get a lot of points for this; most law school exams are open book, so they demand that you do more than just state the law well. You won't get nearly enough points to do well unless you're able to spot issues and make arguments too. But you can't even get started on exams unless you're ready to state the legal doctrines that apply.

Issue Spotting

Before you start discussing anything at all on an exam, you'll have to *spot the issues* that need to be discussed. Looking back at the Belligerist fact pattern, here are questions you might ask—the issues you might spot:

- Can Proctor sue the professor, even though the student (not the professor) attacked her?
- Can Proctor sue the student who attacked her, although the student was temporarily out of control because of the sadistic exam?
- Can the student who attacked Proctor sue the professor for causing the student's own actions?
- Can the student with the anxiety disorder sue the professor, even though he couldn't have known about her condition?
- Can anybody sue the Belligerist website for encouraging the whole thing?

Once you've identified these questions, you'll need to frame each of them in terms of legal doctrines. To do that, of course, you'll need to *know* some legal doctrines.

For example, consider the first question: whether Proctor, who was attacked by an enraged student, can sue the professor. You'll need to know that the relevant legal concept here is *negligence*. (For the time being, you can think of negligence as a failure to take sufficient care to protect someone else.) Once you've taken a class on torts, you'll know that a plaintiff suing for negligence must show that the defendant *caused* the harm. You'll say this in legal language: *Proximate cause is an element of negligence.*

By the time you get to the exam, you'll have studied different rules on proximate cause. These rules appear in what lawyers call "cases"—opinions written by judges to explain why they ruled in favor of one party or another. (The word "case" can mean either the dispute itself or the judicial opinion that explains how it was resolved.) In law school, most of your reading consists of cases, compiled in textbooks called "casebooks."

For example, you might have read the case *In re Polemis*, which says there is a rule that a plaintiff can show negligence only if the defendant directly caused the harm. But you might also have read a case called *Wagon Mound*, which says that there is proximate cause only if the harm was foreseeable. In other words, Proctor doesn't have to show that the professor directly caused her injury—only that the professor should have foreseen it. On law school exams, you'll have to identify the different rules that might apply. You'll say something like this:

> The question is whether the professor proximately caused Proctor's injury. Two rules might apply here. If the *Polemis* rule applies, Proctor must show that the injury was directly caused by the professor's negligence. If the *Wagon Mound* rule applies, Proctor must show that the professor could reasonably have foreseen the injury.

That's issue spotting: framing questions about a fact pattern in terms of the specific legal doctrines you've studied in class.

Notice that when you spot issues on the exam, you're not just identifying one rule. Law school exams frequently present you with situations where more than one rule might apply. You don't go to law school to learn "the law"; you go to law school to learn to identify the multiplicity of rules that might apply to a particular fact pattern.

Exams test you on your ability to work with ambiguity. Most nonlawyers think that legal work is a matter of finding rules and applying them. That's part of it. But legal work involves much more than the simple application of rules. Lawyers often encounter situations where rules conflict, or where rules are ambiguous, or where there are no rules at all.

Sometimes a single legal text could be read to create two different rules. Many law school exams will require you to discuss the different rules that might be seen in a single judicial opinion, or a single piece of statutory text. Clear rules are sometimes found in the law—but they're the easy part of the job, the part you hardly need a law degree to deal with. Ambiguous rules and conflicting rules are what require serious legal thinking. That's what law school exams test.

So a single question—*Can Proctor sue the professor?*—becomes several questions. The first is a question about legal doctrine: which rule should apply, *Polemis* or *Wagon Mound*? Then, for each rule, you'll have to ask how the facts fit the rule: If *Polemis* applies, was Proctor's injury directly caused? If *Wagon Mound* applies, was Proctor's injury foreseeable? You will get points just for identifying these questions. That's issue spotting.

Arguments and Counterarguments

Once you've spotted the issues, you make arguments. On the question of which rule should apply, you might point out that foreseeability is a more widely accepted test than directness. (Your professor told you this in class.) But unless the exam tells you which state you're in, you'll have to discuss and apply each of the rules you've studied in class. Remember: law school exams don't want the *right* answer; they want *all* the possible answers.

For full credit, you'll have to discuss the arguments for and against each approach. You might say, for example, that the foreseeability approach leads to better *consequences*. If people have to pay for unforeseeable injuries, they'll take expensive precautions against extremely unlikely events, which is a bad idea. (We don't, for example, think that the professor should have asked for a battery of psychological tests on each student, to make sure that none of them was likely to attack Proctor. Or do we?) You might also say that the foreseeability rule is more *fair*. It's just not right to hold someone liable for an injury they couldn't have foreseen.

You'll also want to rebut each argument with the best argument for the other side. If you've spotted a genuine issue, every argument has a response, and you'll only get full credit if you identify the response too. Remember: law school exams don't want to know which argument is right; they want the best arguments on *both sides*.

Once you've discussed which rule should apply, you move on to the facts on the exam. You'll have to discuss the analysis that applies under both rules; we may as well start with the *Polemis* directness test. Did the professor directly cause Proctor's injury? The professor will say no: he didn't attack Proctor; the student did. So his negligence was only an indirect cause. Proctor, on the other hand, would argue that the professor *was* the proximate cause of her injuries, because the student was just a puppet on the professor's strings.

Once you've set these arguments and counterarguments out, you've explained the analysis that would apply under one of the two available rules. That's not the end of your discussion. You still have to explain how the analysis would work if the *Wagon Mound* foreseeability doctrine, instead of the *Polemis* directness test, applied. You'll keep going until all possible doctrines have been applied to each of the facts on your exam.

Here's a very important point: you *must* make the counterarguments. You can't just say "If the test is foreseeability, the professor was probably the proximate cause." You have to give the best arguments on both sides: the best argument that the professor could have foreseen the attack on Proctor, *and* the best argument that he couldn't have foreseen it. Then you have to do the same thing with the second doctrine that might apply: make the best case that the professor directly caused the harm to Proctor, and then make the best case that he didn't. A relatively simple question may have four different answers, and you'll need to give all of them.

Once you've applied all of the available rules, you need a conclusion. It'll be something like this: " . . . which is why I think the foreseeability test should apply, and why I think the professor prevails." But your conclusion is usually tentative ("the court would probably find for the defendant"). What really matters isn't which conclusion you reach; it's whether you've spotted all the issues and made all the arguments.

This has been an intentionally simplified discussion of complicated legal doctrines, but even in this simple version you see how the arguments multiply. That's why law school exams are so hard. That's why law is so hard.

IRAC Oversimplifies

Many books on law school will advise you to use an approach to exams called IRAC, which stands for Issue, Rule, Application, and Conclusion. It's a useful way to begin thinking about legal analysis, but it oversimplifies. As you can see from the discussion above, the way to get the most points on an exam is to find places where *more than one rule applies to the facts*. Often, the best way to get points is to discuss which rule should apply, and why. You have to list the various possible rules first, then analyze the case under each of the various rules.

And for many of the rules, you may have to make not just one argument, but counterarguments too. That kind of analysis doesn't fit well into the IRAC structure. IRAC misleadingly suggests that there is only one argument and one conclusion for each issue. If you fail to give counterarguments on law school exams, it is virtually impossible to get a good grade.

IRAC may serve you well in other contexts; it's a perfectly good structure for answering questions on the bar exam, for example, and when you're writing a legal brief or memo, it's helpful to follow the IRAC structure. (You may be surprised how easy it is to forget to come to a conclusion—even that "C" can be a helpful reminder sometimes.) But traditional exam essays often have to use a more complicated structure than IRAC suggests.

Policy Questions

So far we've been talking about traditional law school exam questions, but not all exam questions are issue spotters like the Belligerist example. Many exams feature, as their final question, something called a *policy question*: a question that asks you to analyze the practical implications of the legal doctrines you've studied, or the theoretical arguments for and against those doctrines.

A few professors give a whole exam consisting of a single policy question. A Yale professor in 1939 gave his class an exam that asked them to criticize or defend this proposition: "It is practically useless to pass a pro-labor statute in these United States. The courts will emasculate it. . . . They already have."[1] That was it. But exams that are entirely made up of policy questions like this are unusual; much more common is an exam with mostly issue-spotting questions and a policy question thrown in at the end.

Policy questions require the same three skills as traditional questions—distilling the law, issue spotting, and argument. The issue spotting is a bit harder on policy questions, though. Instead of spotting the issues that arise from a set of facts, you'll spot the issues that arise from a general proposition or general question. But it's still issue spotting. Your job is to frame the question in terms of the doctrines you've discussed in class, and then discuss the arguments and doctrines that might be offered to support each side of the policy question. The trick here is to find out in advance, if possible, whether your professor gives policy questions, so you can practice creating the kind of answer they call for.

Short Answers and Multiple Choice

Two more common variations on the traditional issue spotter are short-answer questions and multiple-choice questions. Again, it's important to find out early in the semester, if possible, whether your exam will include either of these types of question. If it will, you'll need to prepare differently, because the skills you need for short-answer and multiple-choice questions are different from the skills you need for issue spotters: you don't do any issue spotting, and you don't make arguments.

A few exams are entirely short answers, but it's more common to see exams with one big fact-pattern and a few short-answer questions. Many short-answer questions test your distilling skills directly; they require you to understand the law, rather than apply it. For example, you might be asked to simply summarize in one sentence the holding of a case you read during the semester. If you've been doing a good job distilling the law, this will be easy.

Not all short-answer questions test your distilling. Some professors use short-answer questions to test you on the factual or procedural details of important cases; they want to make sure you were paying attention in class. If your professor is going to test you on details, you'll need to take notes in a way that keeps those details readily accessible.

Multiple-choice questions, like short-answer questions, don't test your argument or issue-spotting skills. More likely, they'll test your ability to interpret specific bits of legal language, and your ability to recognize and formulate the doctrines you've studied. The skills that multiple-choice exams require are very specific, and if you're going to face a multiple-choice exam, it's important to practice taking multiple-choice questions.

Some professors are harshly critical of multiple-choice questions. For one thing, multiple-choice questions don't bear much resemblance to the real world; the questions you'll face as a practicing lawyer are never multiple choice. And most law school professors aim to show you how complex and malleable legal concepts are; after a semester of this, multiple-choice questions can seem painfully oversimplified. One professor writes, "I spent all semester telling students that the answer to many legal questions is 'it depends,' and multiple choice exams convey the message that I was lying."[2]

Still, there is an argument for multiple-choice exams: the bar exam is mostly multiple choice. Of course, the criticisms above apply to the bar exam as well: it's not clear why we admit lawyers to the profession based on their skill at answering multiple choice questions, rather than skills that are more likely to be deployed in law practice. Still, the bar exam is a reality, and your professors may feel that they can help you prepare for it by teaching you to answer multiple-choice questions.

If you *do* get a multiple-choice exam, there is a frequently offered piece of advice you should be skeptical of. Many people believe that when you're in doubt about a multiple-choice question, you should go with your first instinct. Psychologists call this the "first-instinct fallacy." A series of studies over seventy-five years has concluded that "[t]he majority of answer changes are from incorrect to correct, and most people who change their answers usually improve their test scores."[3] Why do so many people believe the opposite to be true? Because we remember the mistaken changes better. When you're reviewing an exam you took, and you see that you changed your answer from right to wrong, it stings so much that you don't forget it. On the other hand, when you see that you changed the answer from wrong to right, you're happy—but it's a forgettable experience. The mistakes stick in your head, which eventually creates the illusion that there are more of them.[4] If you're considering changing an answer, go with your better judgment, not your first instinct.

Another kind of exam that's different from traditional exams is the closed-book exam. In most law school exams, you can refer to your notes and your books. But some professors feel that closed-book exams are helpful preparation for the bar exam, because they force you to lodge key bits of doctrine—bits you'll need to reproduce on the closed-book bar exam—deep in your brain. For a closed-book exam, you'll have to memorize the legal doctrines you'll apply. So when you take notes during the semester, you'll want to make them as concise as possible. Again, it's important to find out early in the semester, if you can, whether your exam will be open book or closed book: the notes you take will have to look different, depending on what kind of exam you're facing.

Friendlier Kinds of Grading

Although grades in most classes are based on a single exam at the end of the semester, some professors give midterms. These professors are giving you more than one chance to be measured, and extra feedback on your progress. Be grateful: a professor who gives a midterm is doing a lot of extra work to make your grade more fair and your exams more useful. Midterms don't change anything about the advice this book gives you, except for the timing: you'll have to prepare for two exams, instead of one.

A more dramatic alternative to traditional grading is the system of pass/fail grading used at a few law schools, and in a few classes at some otherwise-traditional law schools. Many of these aren't *really* pass/fail; along with "pass" and "fail," they also have grades like "high pass," so the whole system works out to be pretty similar to curved letter grades at other schools. If you're in a genuine pass/fail class—in which pretty much everybody passes, and nobody gets a "high pass"—your incentives change dramatically. You have the freedom to experiment with different ways of studying. If you use a laptop to take notes in class, try giving it up for a few weeks, and see if you get more out of class discussion, or try other bold experiments. It's a chance to learn how you learn.

Classes That Grade You on Practical Skills

Departing even further from the traditional model, there are some classes that grade you primarily not on an exam, but on other kinds of work you do during the semester. In your first year, you will probably take a course on legal research and writing; your grade in that class may be based on the research and writing assignments you do over the whole semester, rather than on an exam at the end. In some upper-level classes, your grade may be based on a more detailed and lengthy essay or article that you research and write over the course of the semester. You may also take classes that are designed to teach specific practical skills—classes on trial advocacy, negotiation, or other lawyerly skills. Most law schools also offer students the chance to take *clinics*, which are basically law offices that operate within the law school, in which students practice law with real clients under the supervision of faculty members. There are also *externships*, in which students work for off-campus firms and organizations and receive course credit for it. In none of these kinds of courses will your grade be based on a single issue-spotting exam.

Later parts of the book, especially chapter 12 and part 4, will talk in more detail about the skills you'll develop in these nontraditional courses. But you won't be able to do well in any class—traditional or nontraditional—unless you've developed the three skills that traditional exams test: distilling the law, spotting issues, and making arguments. So before we cover the nontraditional classes, we need to finish our discussion of traditional exams, and then to understand the skills they test.

In a survival situation, every decision is important.

United States Air Force Manual 64-3

2 Seven Choices You'll Make on Exam Day

This chapter is about how to take exams. The choices you make on exam day are the choices you're graded on—not your choices about how to prepare for class discussion; not your choices about what to say when your professor calls on you; not your choices about what color highlighter to use in your casebooks. The choices you'll make on exam day are the choices you should be planning for.

This chapter will not give you an exam method. Instead, I'll explain the choices you'll need to make when you take an exam. *You* make the choices. I'll just help you understand what they are, and what's at stake.

Whether to Read the Whole Exam before You Start Writing

Your first decision is whether to begin your work on the exam by reading the whole thing straight through. This depends on how much time you have and how much time you'll need. If you're taking a twenty-four-hour take-home exam, you may as well read the whole thing. You may learn something from reading the whole exam before you start. If you notice that question three is all about, say, the doctrine of transferred intent, then it's pretty unlikely that you need to look for transferred-intent issues in questions one and two.

On the other hand, reading the exam all the way through might be a waste of time you don't have. If you're in a three-hour timed exam, and you're not sure you can finish in time, you might want to read only one question at a time. It might take five minutes to read the second and third questions, and those five minutes are precious.

Whatever you read, of course, it's very important to read carefully. When the proctor says, "OK, open your booklets and begin," adrenaline surges through your body, and you feel as if you're on a Ferris wheel that's just come loose from its moorings. These are not the ideal conditions for reading comprehension. Take deep breaths; read every sentence twice.

How to Structure the Answer

The next choice to make is how to structure your answer. The challenge is breaking big fact patterns into pieces you can work with. Should your answer follow a story in chronological order? Should it discuss each person in the fact pattern, one by one? Or should it follow some other structure? Before you make that decision, look at the *call* of the question. That's the part where the exam tells you what it wants. It usually comes at the very end.

For example, the call might be "Who can sue Mr. Freeze?" It's asking you *who*, so your outline should probably be structured around the people or entities who might be able to sue. Each part of your answer should begin like this: "*Little Timmy* might be able to sue Mr. Freeze, because such-and-such." If the question asks "*What claims* might Geraldo assert against his producer?" then each part of your answer should begin by identifying a claim, rather than a person.

If the call doesn't seem to have a particular structure in mind ("Discuss the legal issues raised by these facts"), look for the structure that makes the most sense. Consider the way the exam itself is structured. If the fact pattern gives you a series of events in chronological order, you might want to structure your answer in chronological order too. Criminal procedure exams, for example, usually tell a story about someone getting arrested and interrogated and charged with a crime. So your analysis should probably follow the order of the story.

Other exams tend to give you a complex set of relationships. In a contracts class, for example, you might have a contract between two corporations, and lots of details about different members of the board of directors, employees, and customers. If your job is to figure out what implications the contract has for each of a dozen people, you might want to organize your answer around *people*; start with one person and discuss the legal consequences for him or her before moving on to the next person.

Still other exams might give you a single fact or law that raises a lot of legal issues. For example, a constitutional law exam might tell you that a particular state law has been passed, and then ask you if it's constitutional. For this question, you might need to organize your answer around the legal issues raised. The law might be unconstitutional because it violates due process, or because it exceeds Congress's authority under the commerce clause, or because it's a bill of attainder, or for a long list of other reasons. The challenge will be to list all the legal issues raised and then discuss them in a sensible, orderly way. It may not matter much what order you put them in.

How to Plan Your Answer

Once you know how your answer will be organized, you'll decide how much time to spend planning and outlining each answer before you begin writing. People will give you lots of advice about this; one book demands you spend twenty minutes organizing your answer, while another insists on a surprisingly specific seven minutes. The right answer will depend on your exam, and on how you work best.

A typical outlining strategy might look like this:

- First, list all of the transactions, or entities, or issues that you need to discuss, following the organization strategy you've chosen.
- Then, for each item on the list, ask yourself what the major legal issues are. Note them.
- Finally, check to see if you've missed anything. Think back over the issues covered in the course.

Checking to see what you've missed is a very important step. We'll talk later about the notes and outlines you'll use to check your work for missing legal issues. For now, note too that it's important to check for missed facts.

If you see a fact that you haven't used, it probably means you've missed an issue. It's very unusual for an exam to contain a fact that doesn't suggest a legal issue of some kind. If the exam tells you that Mr. Tulkinghorn is the brother of Captain Silver, it's because your professor thinks that fact creates a legal problem of some kind. Once in a while, a law professor will put in a purely gratuitous fact as a decoy, but that's rare.

Whether to Cite Cases by Name

Now you start writing. Here's a common question: When you discuss a legal concept (also called a "proposition"), should you mention the name of the case it comes from? You don't want to assault your professor with an endless list of every case covered in the course. But you do want to get all possible points.

Some professors will tell you they don't give credit for naming cases. "I don't care if you know the name of the case," they'll say, "as long as I can see that you understood the doctrine it stands for." Thus Professor White-bread's book on exam taking: "By and large, you should *not* use case names in answering a hypothetical fact pattern essay question. Professors have no interest in your memorizing case names. . . . [Y]ou do not need to know or use case names in your response."[1]

Many professors believe that they don't give their students credit for mentioning case names, but in some cases it's not true. To understand why professors might give points for things they think they don't want, you have to understand competitive grading. Remember that most professors grade exams using a point system. They assign a certain point value to every useful thought that appears in your exam answer. It may seem unfair to the professor to give the same number of points to a student who merely discusses the right legal propositions and to a student who discusses the same propositions *and* mentions the cases they come from. This is why exams sometimes amount to mentioning contests, in which the most points go to the student who mentions the most relevant legal propositions and arguments. If you're not sure what the professor wants, mention the case name.

This advice won't work for all professors. There are a few who mean it when they say they don't want you to use case names. In one class I took, the exam was only nine questions, and each of our answers was limited to three sentences. That professor didn't want us to name cases, and he wasn't kidding. The best guide to what a professor wants is her past exams and the essays that received high grades—if they're available.

An important note: even if you decide it's better to mention case names, it's important to be selective. The professor will probably get annoyed if your exam contains a list of every case in your casebook. It's usually wise to stick to the cases that were mentioned by name in class. And it's very important to avoid using case names as a substitute for the legal concepts embodied in those cases. For example, you should never just say "the rule adopted in the *Polemis* case" without also saying what that rule was. That way, the professor can see that you've done your distilling—that you understand the rules you're talking about well enough to express them in your own words.

Whether to Discuss Reasoning and Policy

Each exam will require you to decide how much depth to go into. When you discuss a case, how much detail should you give? Should you discuss the reasoning of the case? ("The *Clenis* case held that if Congress had wanted to create an exception to the statute's plain language, it would have said so.") Should you discuss the policy issues raised by the fact patterns you face? ("The court should reject this argument because it would give too much discretion to police officers, who are not institutionally competent to decide important social policy questions; and also because it would incentivize cat-juggling . . .")

It depends on what your professor wants. Here you can probably rely on the advice your professor gives you during class discussion. She probably knows whether she wants to hear discussions of reasoning or policy. But the best guide is prior exams, if they're available. When I took my constitutional law professor's old exam, for practice, I finished in about half the allotted time, and couldn't think of anything else to say. Then I looked at the old answers on file. They discussed the cases in about three times as much depth as I had. That's what the professor wanted. The exam looked just like any other exam. But it wanted a level of depth that my other exams didn't even approach. You'll need to understand what your professor wants.

Whether to Say What's Obvious

Another challenge is to figure out when you need to mention things that seem completely obvious. In a constitutional law class, you might be asked to analyze the constitutionality of a statute that prohibits throwing Slurpees at moving cars.

You've learned lots of doctrines under which a statute might be unconstitutional, and you write an exam answer that covers most of them. But then you stop to puzzle over whether to mention the due process doctrine, under which a statute can be unconstitutional because it's arbitrary and irrational. Only an idiot could think that it's arbitrary or irrational to outlaw throwing Slurpees at cars. Do you really need to talk about this?

Again, the answer is to do whatever will get you the most points. You probably won't lose points for stating the obvious, so state it. On the other hand, you'll lose precious time, and test the professor's patience, if you discuss an obvious point at unnecessary length. So probably the best approach is to say, "It's entirely rational to ban Slurpee throwing, so this does not violate the right to due process." Leave it at that. Chances are you'll get a point, and rightly so: you've shown your professor that you're thinking of all possible problems.

Another reason to mention the obvious: sometimes you'll start writing a sentence like that and realize that it's *not* so obvious after all. Many things that seem obvious aren't.

What You'll Do Afterward

The normal feeling that comes right after an exam isn't relief; it's agonized self-doubt. You'll think you missed everything important. Worse, you'll hear other students talking about the exam and realize they spotted something you missed. Remember that most exams are designed so that everyone will miss something—you're not supposed to get all the answers. Even the best exam in the class usually misses something.

Remember what Abraham Lincoln said to a friend immediately after the Gettysburg Address: "It is a flat failure, and the people are disappointed."[2] In the comedown after a major trial and the rush of adrenaline that goes with it, we are not the best judges of our own performance. Try to put the exam behind you and get ready for the next one.

If you're feeling too burnt out to get ready for your next exam, you might want to try searching the web for pictures of cute baby animals. According to one of the sweetest psychological studies ever conducted, people who had recently looked at pictures of adorable puppies were better at tasks that required careful attention.[3]

Then ensued a scene of riot and carnage such as no human pen, or steel one either, could describe. People were shot, probed, dismembered, blown up, thrown out of the window. There was a brief tornado of murky blasphemy, with a confused and frantic wardance glimmering through it, and then all was over. In five minutes there was silence, and the gory chief and I sat alone and surveyed the sanguinary ruin that strewed the floor around us.

He said, "You'll like this place when you get used to it."

MARK TWAIN, *Journalism in Tennessee*

3 What You'll Need by Exam Day

The last chapter listed the decisions you'll make when you take an exam. Many of them can be made before you walk into the exam room. So you'll want to develop a plan for each exam. By "plan" I don't mean an elaborate written document; what you need is just a basic working sense of how you're going to approach each exam.

You'll also need to be in practice. Exam taking is a skill, and you can't start cold on exam day. This chapter will give you some ideas about how to get into practice in the run-up to exam day.

Finally, you'll need the law at your fingertips. You'll want to review your notes from the semester, and you'll also want to have an outline ready for quick reference during the exam. This chapter ends with a few words on how notes and outlines help you on exams.

A Plan

To plan for an exam, you'll consult three main resources: old exams on file, your professor's advice, and the exams you've taken in other classes in the past.

The most important of these is your professor's prior exams and sample answers to those exams. Some schools make available to students previous exams given by the professor and the highest-scoring student's answer. (Or in some cases sample answers written by the professor.) Other schools don't make these available to students, which is unfortunate. The point of looking at them is *not* to see what material they cover—professors may change their syllabi from year to year, so there's no guarantee that the material will be the same. Instead, the point of looking at old exams is to see how your professor prefers students make the decisions listed in the last chapter. Do the best exams cite a lot of cases by name? Do they discuss reasoning and policy? Do they mention points that are glaringly obvious?

To answer these questions, look at the old exams early in the semester. I mean really early, like the first or second week. That way, you can see what the best answers look like—how many cases they cite, whether they discuss reasoning or policy in detail, whether they mention obvious points—*before* you do the semester's work of taking notes. If the best answers discuss cases in depth, for example, you'll need to take notes accordingly. But if the best answers mention cases quickly and then move on, you'll want to take notes that prepare you to do the same.

As you look at these old exams, remember that the point of law school exams isn't to get the answers "right." The best exam from last year might have said one thing, but if you've reached the opposite conclusion, you might well have gotten full credit too. There are at least two plausible answers to any interesting legal question. You're looking at the old exams to see what kind of strategy they reward, not to see what substantive answers the best exam taker gave.

Some professors encourage students to think about exams early and often. At my school, there was a rule that professors had to discuss the exam on the first day of class. But a word of warning is appropriate here: some professors don't like to see students digging through old exams early in the semester. They want to see students immersing themselves in the law, not grubbing for grades. Is that fair? On one hand, law schools have chosen to assess students' performance on the basis of a single long exam, and there's nothing unseemly about students recognizing that fact and focusing their work accordingly. Law school gives you no choice but to start thinking about exams early. On the other hand, professors are right to feel annoyed if students seem not to care about the law except as it relates to the exam. You're in law school to learn how to speak and think about the law, not just to get good grades. So start your exam preparations early, but be careful about how you involve professors in that process.

Another source of the information you'll use to plan for exams is the professor herself. Your professor is a useful but not completely trustworthy source of information about the exam and how to do well on it. When she describes the exam, you and everyone in the class will stop playing solitaire on your laptops and pay careful attention, and rightly so. But be suspicious. As chapter 2 explained, professors may think they don't give points for something, but end up giving points for it anyway. Compare what she says with her old exams, if you can.

The exams that you yourself took in previous semesters are the third resource you'll need. (Obviously, this isn't possible in your first semester.) Developing a plan for exam taking isn't just about learning how your professor works—it's also about learning how *you* work. After exams are over and you've gotten your grades, most professors will post the exams and a sample answer. Review them, and your own exam, carefully.

This is usually a painful experience. Prepare to forgive yourself for oversights that seem obvious in retrospect (everything seems obvious in retrospect), as well as bad writing (nobody writes well under time pressure) and all the other mistakes everyone makes in the frantic scrabble of exam day. The pain is worth it. Few things will do more to help you get better grades the next time.

Reviewing your old exams is how you assess your own performance. Compare your exam to the sample answer; try to see where you got points. Try to understand where your strategy helped you and where it didn't. Talk to your professor. Ask how you could have done better. The process of reviewing old exams and rethinking your exam strategy is where you'll get some of your best ideas about which approaches work best for you.

By the way, this isn't just a good approach to exams. The ability to look back on your own performance with a cool eye, and reflect on what could have worked better, is priceless for any kind of work. It's how you learn.

Practice

Exam taking is a skill. It can only be learned with practice. Exam taking doesn't much resemble the other kinds of work you do over the semester. It requires you to develop a sustained legal analysis on paper under time pressure. You don't normally do that in class. So you'll need to practice.

The last section suggested you look at your professor's old exams early in the semester. Later, as the exam approaches, you'll want to get those old exams out again, and actually *take* them. Sit down and work through them, and time yourself. The goal is not to see what material was covered on the old exam—you can get a better sense of what will be on your exam simply by noticing what your professor spent the most time discussing. Instead, the goal is to answer the other questions listed in the last chapter: Should you start by reading the whole exam through? How much time should you spend planning and outlining? How should you outline?

It's important that you take the old exams under time pressure; use a clock and time yourself. To figure out how much time you should spend planning and outlining, for example, you'll need to know how much time pressure there'll be. You'll also need a sense of how you respond to this particular professor's exams under time pressure. Some professors write exams that are designed to take only a fraction of the time allotted, so that students can think carefully and reflect on their answers. Others write exams that will require you to type as fast as you can for the entire three hours. You can only get a sense of this by taking practice exams under timed conditions.

Practice is only effective if it's accompanied by *thinking*. As you take practice exams, spend some time thinking about the sample answers, and how your practice sessions went. Ask yourself what you could have done better. Assess your strategy. Did you start writing too fast? Or did you spend too much time outlining? Did you run out of steam at the end when it was time to check your work? What worked well?

Remember that the old exams may not cover the same material as your exam. The professor may have taught the course differently in previous years. So you might bungle some questions even if you've understood every word of your class. Don't worry about that. The point is to get practice and develop your strategy, not to get the substantive answers right.

If there are no old exams available for you to look at, you're at a disadvantage. It'll be harder to figure out what your professor wants. If your professor doesn't give you old exams, ask her if there's another professor whose exams she thinks would be useful for practice. If she can't help you, go find some exam in the same subject and take it. Even if there are large sections you don't understand, because your class didn't cover the same material, you need to practice writing exams in each subject to get the feel of it. Other people's exams are better than nothing.

Although taking old exams is the best way to practice, there are other useful ways of getting your brain into exam mode. Of course, some of these can be time consuming, so it's important to choose carefully, but it's also important to keep experimenting. What works best for you might be something unconventional. For example, you might try to write an exam of your own. Think about how you would structure an exam that forced students to grapple with the major issues you've studied. What would it look like? If you have old exams, try to structure it the same way they're structured, but come up with your own fact pattern. If you don't have any old exams, try different structures for the questions, and see what works best.

A less work-intensive version of the same approach would be to simply try to guess what subjects are going to appear on your exam. Make a list of substantive legal issues you think the professor might cover, or a list of policy questions. Thinking from the professor's perspective in this way can lead to two good things happening. First, you'll learn to see the law the way your professor does—as a conceptual whole, rather than as a long and disparate list of cases. As the next chapter will explain, seeing the course as one big conceptual structure is a key part of understanding the law. Creating your own exam questions also helps you see the exam as your professor does—as a place to hide legal issues.

Second, you may actually guess right. It's very difficult for professors to write law school exams year after year without repeating themselves. And if your professor has given you enough hypotheticals in class, you can probably start to see what kind of hypotheticals appeal to her. My study group often joked about how sure we were that our constitutional law professor would have an exam question about the Congressional resolution that authorized the use of force in Iraq (this was fall 2002), because it came up so often in class. She clearly thought it illustrated a lot of the principles we'd been discussing. Sure enough, half the exam was on the Iraq use-of-force resolution.

Your Notes and Outline

Along with practicing your exam skills, you'll need to get your understanding of the law in shape. One excellent way to get ready for the exam is to edit your notes. I say *edit* your notes, instead of *review* them, because reviewing works better if you do it actively. Don't just read your notes; mess with them. Rename entries, reorganize the structure, and generally tinker until you feel they are a good reflection of the material.

By tinkering, you are interacting, and you learn more when you're interacting. Editing makes you much more familiar with the material than just reading it. Things you've recently distilled, or redistilled, stay fresh in your mind.

The most important tool you'll need on exam day is your outline. An outline is an overview of the major topics covered in the class. During the exam—this is critical—the outline functions as a checklist.

Each class covers only a finite number of legal concepts. So there's a fairly short list of concepts that could be hiding in any exam fact pattern. To spot issues successfully, you should have that list, on paper, with you during the exam. (If you have a closed-book exam, you'll have to memorize the list, maybe scribbling it down onto scrap paper when the exam starts.)

In a contracts class, for example, you might have three basic units: the elements of a contract; defenses to contract claims; and remedies for breaches of contract. Within each unit, there will be a few more issues. In the unit on defenses to contract, you might cover incompetence, duress, mistake, misrepresentation, justified nonperformance, and unconscionability. If you bring to the exam a list of these concepts—a short list—you can use it as an issue-spotting checklist.

As you analyze an exam, you'll spot all the issues you can, but you'll worry that you may be missing some. So you look over at your list of the issues covered in the class, and check off the ones you've already spotted. If there are issues covered in class that you haven't spotted on the exam, check again. *We spent a lot of time on duress,* you might think to yourself, *but I don't see how anyone in this fact pattern is under duress.* Now that you know what you're looking for, you notice that a big company has been threatening a small company with blacklisting. Is that economic duress? Now you've spotted the issue.

Of course, not every exam covers every issue. But most professors try to write an exam that covers as much of the course material as possible. So the professors do, in effect, just what you're doing: they look back at a list of issues covered in the class and try to fit them into the exam. Your checklist of issues—your course outline—will often be your key to seeing the exam as the professor sees it. Chapter 11 will explain how outlines work.

This overview of how outlines work should be comforting. Exams are frightening, but it's good news that exams will test you on a finite list of concepts. The material you cover in law school classes can seem endless and bottomless, but it isn't. You don't have to know everything—you have to know just enough to take the test. No matter how much time you spend, you'll never *really* understand constitutional law; there's just too much to learn. But that's OK. Nobody *really* understands constitutional law. Your job is to sit down, read an exam, and make some plausible arguments about the limited set of issues you cover in class.

The next part of the book will explain the skills that make that possible.

During the 1870's[,] the West Publishing Company systematically undertook to publish all the opinions handed down by the federal courts, the highest state courts, and, in increasing number, lower state courts.

Whether the West Publishing Company, like the discoverer of the atom bomb, should be looked on as a benefactor of mankind or as an enemy of the human race is a problem of moral philosophy with which a lawyer is ill equipped to deal.

GRANT GILMORE, *The Yale Law Journal*

PART II

The Skills You'll Need

This part of the book explains the three skills that are taught in traditional law school courses. The first skill is *distilling* the law: organizing large quantities of legal information into usable form. The second skill is *issue spotting*: identifying relevant legal questions. The third skill is *argument*: articulating the best legal answers on both sides of the questions you've identified. These three skills are what your professors mean when they talk about "legal reasoning" and "thinking like a lawyer." They're not the only skills lawyers need; part 4 will talk about some others. But they are the skills that traditional exams test.

[W]hatever one may say in praise of Our Lady of the Common Law (to whom I do bow), clarity and precise outline of her rules of law are not the chief jewel in her crown.

KARL LLEWELLYN

4   Distilling the Law

The ability to filter information is a critical cognitive function. According to one version of the Batman story, the reason the Joker acts so crazily is that he can't filter the information his brain receives.[1] In the real world, an inability to filter information—to "distinguish signal from noise"—can be a symptom of schizophrenia, although it doesn't usually lead to clown-themed crime sprees.[2] As a law student, you'll have to perform feats of information filtering that are an order of magnitude more difficult than what ordinary people do in daily life. Or, at least, it'll seem that way at first.

Law school will require you to read a variety of legal texts: constitutions, statutes, regulations, and scholarly commentary. The most common kind of text you'll read is judicial opinions. Judicial opinions are issued by courts when they decide how to rule in a particular case. (As mentioned in chapter 1, lawyers often refer to judicial opinions as "cases," although strictly speaking the case is what the judicial opinion resolves.) When litigants disagree about what the law is, judicial opinions explain whose interpretation of the law prevailed, and why.

The law on which you will be tested is in these texts. But getting the law *out* of the texts is difficult, and not just because they're badly written. Different texts contradict each other. Individual texts are maddeningly ambiguous. Judicial opinions ramble on for many pages, sometimes without ever saying anything that sounds like a rule.

To get the law from these texts, you will have to *distill* them. Distilling is the skill of turning a long, difficult legal text into a single, well-articulated legal concept. When you read a judicial opinion, or a passage from a statute, or the fine print in a contract, and try to articulate for yourself what it means, you're distilling. Everything depends on this skill.

Some students begin law school with a superstitious belief that somewhere there is a giant book in which The Law is written—and if only professors would simply tell us what the Book says, we could avoid reading all these irritatingly murky legal texts that never quite say it clearly. Unfortunately, there is no Book. The murky texts are all we have. They're what law is made of. Distilling them is the first thing you'll need to learn.

Many professors don't talk much about how distilling works. Several of my professors were fond of saying, "My exam assumes you *know* the law; it only tests whether you can *apply* it." Which was like saying, "I assume you can juggle knives; the exam will test whether you can do it on a unicycle while I throw grenades at you." This chapter explains how distilling—the process by which one comes to "know" the law—works.

The Legal Proposition

To understand distilling, you must first understand what you're distilling. The unit of information with which lawyers work is the *legal proposition*. A legal proposition is a single concept, like "the speed limit on Western Avenue is thirty-five miles per hour" or "the Constitution should be interpreted in light of its original meaning."

Legal propositions are the material you'll use to construct your exam answers. They're found in every kind of text you encounter in law school: cases, constitutions, statutes, administrative regulations, treaties, law review articles, and the parts of your casebooks that are written by the editors. When you read, you're hunting for propositions. They're the legal ideas you'll need to have ready when you take the exam.

There are different kinds of propositions. Students sometimes don't see just how many different kinds of propositions they can be tested on. So I'm going to give you an overview of the different kinds of propositions.

THE BLACK-LETTER PROPOSITION

One important category of propositions is propositions of legal doctrine. These are often called *black-letter law*. According to the Oxford English Dictionary Online, the phrase "black letter" refers to the pompous typeface once used "for fancy printing in England," 𝔴𝔥𝔦𝔠𝔥 𝔩𝔬𝔬𝔨𝔢𝔡 𝔰𝔬𝔪𝔢𝔱𝔥𝔦𝔫𝔤 𝔩𝔦𝔨𝔢 𝔱𝔥𝔦𝔰. In law school, "black-letter law" means a legal rule or doctrine, as opposed to all the other things you find in judicial decisions and other legal texts. (We'll talk about what those other things are shortly.) When your grandparents talk about "the law," they mean the black-letter law.

Here are some examples of black-letter propositions:

> When a trespasser knows there are booby-traps on a person's land, and trespasses anyway, the trespasser can't sue the landowner for injuries from the booby-traps.[3]

> It's a crime to travel between states "for the purpose of engaging in any illicit sexual conduct with another person."[4]

> Classified information must be shared only on a need-to-know basis.[5]

The first of these propositions comes from a judicial opinion. The second comes from a statute. The third comes from an executive order issued by the president of the United States. Each of them is "law." These are the kinds of propositions you'll focus on in traditional first-year classes.

Note that black-letter rules are often ambiguous or vague. *Black letter* does not mean *clear*. For example, what is a "need to know" basis? (Who needs to know?) It's a felony to mishandle classified information, so it's important to know exactly what this black-letter proposition means. Interpreting ambiguous propositions like these is the most important intellectual job lawyers do. When you see an ambiguous rule, don't think *what a pain*. Think *ah, this is what I'm here to study*. This was a favorite observation of my torts professor, Girardeau Spann, who never tired of saying, "Remember: You like ambiguity. You're happy about ambiguity."

LEGAL PROPOSITIONS CAN INCLUDE FACTS

Propositions of black-letter law aren't the only kind of proposition you'll need to reproduce on exams. Another kind of proposition, rather than just stating a legal rule, explains how a legal rule applies to a given set of facts. Understanding a legal rule often requires understanding how courts have applied it. Law students often think they're supposed to be learning *rules*, exclusively. But rules are meaningless unless you know how they're applied.

For example, in torts class, you'll study cases involving negligence—meaning cases in which someone is injured because of someone else's failure to take a precaution of some kind. One of the basic questions in this area of law is how much care people should take to avoid harming other people. The general rule is that a person is liable for negligence if she fails to exercise the degree of care that would be taken by a reasonable person under the circumstances. We can distill that down to a short proposition: *there is a duty of reasonable care.* This is an extremely important legal proposition, and you should certainly write it down in your notes. But what does it mean? You'll need specific examples to figure that out.

Say you read a case that says a travel agent was negligent because she booked someone a trip to a resort that was (1) still under construction, and (2) infested with "large red insects."[6] Now you have an example of what it means not to take reasonable care. And you can distill it down to a terse, useful proposition: *If resort is unfinished and infested, travel agent failed to take "reasonable care."* When you get to the exam, and you see a question in which someone fails to investigate something and someone else gets hurt, you'll compare the facts on the exam to these facts.

Notice what we're doing here: We're treating the facts as part of the law. This is a central feature of how American courts work: when they're confronted by a new case, they look to old cases—not just what the old cases said, but the facts involved as well. In effect, the facts of prior cases are part of the law that binds future courts. When lawyers argue about whether a rule should apply to their case, they argue about whether the factual situation in the earlier case was similar to their case, or different in some key way. You can't make that kind of argument without knowing the facts of the earlier case.

BEYOND RULES

Some of the most important propositions you'll learn in law school aren't "rules"—at least, not in the sense of "rule" that suggests a clear, straightforward doctrine that can be applied to a given case without much confusion. (The proposition that American presidents must be at least thirty-five years old is an example of a rule.) When I started law school, I was dismayed to find that many legal propositions aren't rules at all. Instead, they're vague, flexible standards. Family law, for example, tells judges to do whatever is in the "best interests of the child." *That's not a rule,* I muttered—*that hardly even qualifies as advice!*

While some laws seem to create clear, firm rules, like "the speed limit is fifty-five miles per hour," others create vague, imprecise *standards*, like the Fifth Amendment to the US Constitution: "No person shall be . . . deprived of life, liberty, or property, without due process of law."[7] What does "due process of law" mean? The only way to find out is to read the long series of judicial opinions that interpret it. Rules give clear guidance. Standards don't. But both kinds of propositions are black-letter law, and both can be on your exam.

Law students want clarity. Rules are satisfyingly clear; standards are maddeningly vague. But clarity is not the only virtue that matters to lawmakers. Lawmakers might choose to create a standard, rather than a rule, because they want judges' decisions to be sensitive to consequences and justice in individual cases. A crystal-clear, bright-line rule is an inflexible rule. There's often a risk that bright-line rules will create bad results in situations nobody can foresee. Standards allow sensible decisions in situations that are hard to predict.

Consider the Fourth Amendment, which prohibits "unreasonable searches and seizures." The framers of the Constitution wisely chose not to list all of the kinds of searches they thought were unreasonable. As society changes, and technology develops, new kinds of searches come before the courts. The framers couldn't have known that police would someday be able to look through walls, or down from helicopters. So it's fortunate that they created a standard, rather than a rule—leaving it to future courts to decide what's "unreasonable" and what isn't.

Some legal propositions are even less rule-ish. Here's an example. In a criminal case, the judge is supposed to tell the jury that the defendant is presumed innocent. When the judge doesn't, should the defendant get a new trial? The Supreme Court has said that a failure to explain the presumption of innocence

> must be evaluated in light of the *totality of the circumstances*—including all the instructions to the jury, the arguments of counsel, whether the weight of the evidence was overwhelming, *and other relevant factors*.[8]

Propositions like these—which set forth analyses based on factors, rather than standards or rules—can be infuriating, but they have their uses.[9] It's wise for the Supreme Court to create a totality-of-the-circumstances test when it isn't sure what kind of factors should be relevant to the decision. Lower courts can then apply the totality-of-the-circumstances analysis in ways that seem to fit each new case, letting the law develop slowly, and letting the needs of each situation guide the law's growth.

And notice that even though this proposition is slippery and vague, it doesn't give judges *unlimited* discretion. It tells judges, for example, that a failure to instruct the jury about the presumption of innocence can't just be ignored. So a totality-of-the-circumstances proposition does at least take certain options off the table.

Obviously, the distinction between rules and standards isn't absolute. Few laws give unlimited discretion to the people who enforce them. And on the other hand, there are some situations in which any judge will find an exception to even the clearest-looking rule. The speed limit, for example, sounds absolute, but does anyone really drive fifty-five miles per hour? And no matter how clear the text of the law is, would a police officer ticket someone rushing to the hospital if there was a woman giving birth in the car? Virtually all rules leave room for some discretion, at least implicitly.

Many students assume they've come to law school to learn rules, because they assume that law *is* rules. But rules are just one kind of law. Black-letter law can be vague. And vague propositions can be tested on your exam.

PROPOSITIONS OF BAD LAW

Another important thing to understand about legal propositions is that not all of the propositions you'll study turn out to be "good law." A rule is "good law" if it applies in a given jurisdiction and nobody's overruled it yet. The rules you study might have been overruled; or they might not apply in some jurisdictions. These propositions of "bad law" are still testable.

Sometimes you study old rules to see how the law has changed. The US Supreme Court and state supreme courts can overturn their earlier cases. So some of the propositions you study are already wrong—in the sense of not being binding law anywhere—when you learn them. In fact, some propositions are studied precisely *because* they're wrong. You might encounter the infamous 1927 case of *Buck v. Bell*, in which the otherwise-great judge Oliver Wendell Holmes upheld the forced sterilization of a mentally disabled woman, writing: "Three generations of imbeciles are enough."[10] It's a terrible opinion that serves as a frightening menu of ways that law can go wrong. Holmes says, for example, "The principle that sustains compulsory vaccination is broad enough to cover cutting the Fallopian tubes." Why on earth would that be true? It's a great example of how analogical reasoning can go wrong when you fail to explain *why* the two things you're comparing are alike. (And the truth is even more awful than the opinion shows you—Carrie Buck, the young woman whose sterilization the Supreme Court upheld, wasn't even mentally disabled, and her lawyer colluded with her doctors to make sure her sterilization would be upheld.[11]) For just that reason, it's very important to study.

Even more commonly, you'll study rules that don't apply in all of the states. In areas of law where the primary responsibility for lawmaking rests with state governments, rather than the federal government, it sometimes happens that a majority of states choose one rule, while a substantial minority of states choose a contradictory rule. It's important to learn both, because law school professors love to test you on issues where more than one rule might apply.

PROPOSITIONS OF THEORY AND POLICY

Some of the propositions you'll study aren't law at all; they're ideas from fields like philosophy, economics, and political science, which overlap with the study of law. In law school, you won't just learn what the law is; you'll talk about whether it's justified, which means drawing on ideas from political philosophy and related fields. And you'll also talk about the effects that legal rules have, which means drawing from economics and psychology: What incentives will rules create? How do people respond to rules in the real world? You'll also talk about the nature of law. For example, you may talk about the way people often criticize judges for injecting politics into their decisions. What exactly does this mean? If there is a difference between law and politics, what is it? Effective lawyers need to make arguments about all these things, so it's good that you study them in law school. And if you tune out when the discussion turns to theory or social policy, as many students do, you'll miss some of the most important parts of law school—and information you'll need on the exam.

To give you a sense of the kinds of propositions I'm talking about, here are two propositions that try to answer the philosophical question, *what is law?*

Law is the combination of rules about conduct with rules about which rules are legitimate.[12]

Law is a system of narratives.[13]

And here are two conflicting propositions about judging—specifically, what judges should do when they have to choose between two plausible interpretations of an ambiguous legal provision:

A judge interpreting an ambiguous legal rule should try to choose the interpretation that seems best "from the standpoint of political morality."[14]

A judge interpreting an ambiguous legal rule should not think at all about political morality. Judges have no authority to pursue "broader social purposes."[15]

Other propositions you might encounter deal with the *effects* or consequences of legal rules. Here's a proposition that deals with the real-world consequences of trying to ban a particular activity:

A lawmaker deciding whether to outlaw an activity should first think about what people will substitute for it. "There are substitute ways to do almost anything."[16]

All of these propositions are fair game in a law school class. Some students react to philosophical or policy-related propositions like these with irritation, because they think that philosophy and social policy won't be relevant on the exam. But that's a mistake. Law school exams sometimes do include policy questions, like "What is the purpose of contracts law?"

And in legal practice, propositions of policy and theory are sometimes very relevant. When a state supreme court has to decide whether to adopt a new rule of contract law, for example, it usually considers whether the rule would help or hurt the people of the state. A good lawyer knows how to participate in that conversation.

Propositions of theory and policy are potentially testable, just like the propositions of black-letter law you distill from cases. The habit of tuning out discussions of theory and policy is common, and dangerous. Law students sometimes think that any discussion that doesn't involve black-letter law is a tangent. They know exams are looming, and they're not clear on how theory or policy could help them with the exam, so they tune out when the conversation goes in that direction.

If your professor spends time on something, she probably thinks it's relevant to the course. That means she'll give points to students who write about it on her exam. Distill the ideas that emerge from discussions of policy and principle and record them in your notes, just like the black-letter propositions. Resist the urge to put down your pen when your professor starts talking policy.

I don't mean that all professors want to hear about theory and policy on your exam. Some don't. The exam will test your understanding of the course *as the professor presents it.* In your corporations class, your professor might say "I don't care what the law *should be* or whether this all makes sense as a policy matter; I'm trying to teach you to draft a corporate charter and avoid getting sued by shareholders." Don't bother putting policy propositions on that exam.

But in your contracts class, you might spend a lot of time talking about whether, as a matter of justice, the law should enforce agreements that are unfair to one of the parties. You might talk about what commentators from Germany, France, and ancient Rome thought about that question, and then cover a few modern scholars too.[17] If your class spends time on something, it's probably relevant to the exam. Don't dismiss it just because it's not black-letter law.

You Are the Author of the Law

Now that we've seen how many different kinds of propositions you can be responsible for learning, we can discuss how to learn them. Distilling the propositions well involves more than just writing down the legal ideas you find in your casebook. I'm going to suggest, in this section, that good distilling requires you to do four things: First, put the propositions into your own words. Second, test your understanding of the propositions by applying them to new fact patterns. Third, put the propositions into context to see how they fit into the course as a whole. And, fourth, disregard the propositions that don't matter.

COMPOSE THE PROPOSITIONS YOURSELF

The most important thing I can tell you about how to learn legal propositions is *put them in your own words.* Distilling the law isn't a matter of simply extracting the propositions from the cases you read. You yourself have to compose a proposition that aptly summarizes each case.

The texts you study in law school are cryptic, ambiguous, complex, and sometimes incoherent. They don't explain themselves. Most of the cases you read can be interpreted in a number of ways. So you'll have to interpret them. You'll have to reach a conclusion of your own about what they mean before you can apply them to the unfamiliar facts on the exam. That's what you're in law school to learn: *interpreting the law for yourself.* Paraphrasing gets you started.

When you reach the end of a paragraph of especially glutinous judicial prose, stop. Ask yourself, "What did that paragraph say?" Try to paraphrase it out loud. If you succeed, the proposition will stick in your head. If you don't, you'll know you have more thinking to do before you're ready to apply that proposition on an exam. Putting the propositions in your own words is the only way to make sure that you're actually learning. When you rephrase a concept in your own words, your brain engages. That feeling that you get when you're trying to summarize something complicated—that feeling of groping for the next word—is what it feels like to internalize a difficult idea.

Exams will ask you to explain the law in your own words, so you should get into the habit of explaining the law in your own words during the semester. This is why professors ask students to summarize cases in class discussion: they're trying to get you to realize that the basic skill you need, the one on which all others depend, is the ability to read a legal text and restate its meaning in your own words.

I don't mean to say that you have to use your own words for everything. The specific words of statutes, for example, are very important, and you'll often want them in your notes. Some cases, similarly, contain specific phrases that your professors will expect you to know. (You'll be able to tell which phrases are this important by the amount of time your professor spends quoting, and trying to deconstruct the quotes, in class.) But whenever you want to understand something—even if it's a formula whose exact words you memorize—putting it into your own words is crucial. Use the statute's words *and* summarize them in your own words.

You can't make sense of the exam using the propositions as you find them in your casebooks. On the exam, you will rely on the versions of the propositions that you yourself create. Your notes are where you create the version of the law that you'll use on the exam.

Be wary of study systems that don't involve actually formulating your own version of the law. In particular, be wary of the five-colored highlighting system that some books recommend, which involves using a different-colored highlighter for the facts of a case, its holding, its reasoning, and so on. Many people use this system, and it does have some advantages. For one thing, it can help you follow class discussion: when the professor asks someone to describe the facts of a case, you'll know to look for the blue sentences—which is helpful even if you're not the one being called on. But highlighting each sentence in a case takes time, and it's important to ask what you get from that investment.

The problem with the multicolored highlighting system is that for some students, it functions as a substitute for distilling: they highlight the cases instead of summarizing them in notes. But highlighting is *passive*; it involves categorizing things, not struggling to explain and understand them. You learn the law by putting it into your own words. Highlighting can't substitute for real distilling.

Some students who use the highlighting system use it to help them refer to casebooks during exams; sometimes they write their distilled version of the propositions in the margins. But this approach can be time consuming; flipping open the casebook and scanning the margins for the distilled proposition takes time, which you don't have much of during an exam. And if you've distilled the propositions in the margins of your casebook, instead of in your notes, you're less likely to come back to the propositions later to revise them and tinker with them. Tinkering can be one of the best ways to study for an exam, because editing propositions is a much better way to get them into your brain than just reading them repeatedly.

Note that although it's important to state the propositions in your own words, it's also important to make sure that your version of the law doesn't look too different from your professor's version. If your professor doesn't recognize the proposition you're reciting on an exam, you won't get credit for it. So in some ways, your work over the semester will be an attempt to construct a version of the law that looks as much like your professor's as possible. But you must create it yourself, proposition by proposition. The law you're tested on looks like your professor's, but it's still *your law.* You compose it.

WIGGLE THE PROPOSITIONS TO SEE WHERE THEY HURT

The process of distilling doesn't end when you put the propositions into your own words. You'll need to understand how the propositions apply to specific fact patterns. To understand the law, you have to practice applying it to new sets of facts. By the time the exam comes around, you'll need to have internalized the propositions and the way they relate to each other. You'll need to have information ready and available for immediate, confident use under high pressure during the exam. The propositions will be ready for you if you've practiced applying them already.

It's like the way a sprained foot tempts you to wiggle it around to see exactly where it hurts. That's what learning is like: you wiggle the proposition around to see where it hurts.

Try to internalize the questioning process that happens in class. Your brain should develop the habit of probing and testing each proposition the way your professors do, to see if you understand its implications and its limits. When your professor says that being forced to say the Pledge of Allegiance in school is unconstitutional, you should think, What if I was only forced to *listen* to it? What if it was an extracurricular club, not the school itself, that required me to say it? And so on. Your brain will get good at doing this automatically, if you practice.

When you write things down in your notes, you'll sometimes get the shaky feeling that you're just transcribing someone else's words, rather than actually understanding them. Sometimes when you look back at your notes you'll feel a little numbness in your brain, a little question mark. Your brain is telling you that you don't quite know what that proposition means.

When you get that feeling, stop. Ask yourself if you really understand the proposition. Summarize the rule back to yourself, out loud. Turn your chapter titles into questions to see just how much you've actually learned. If you have a unit on "Grand Jury Secrecy," ask yourself, What part of what a grand jury does is secret? And, Who is it secret from? And, why? See how far your understanding goes.

The most valuable thinking you do about reading is in the moments after you finish, when you stare off into space and ask yourself, What does this mean? What did I think of that case? Would I have decided it differently? Why? Learn to daydream well.

SEEING THE WHOLE CATHEDRAL

Learning to distill cases into individual propositions is challenging, but it's just the beginning. The exam won't test you on whether you can summarize particular cases. Instead, it'll ask you to apply the whole system of law that you learn in each class to a new set of facts. So it takes more than a list of legal propositions to make sense of an exam.

To apply the propositions to the fact patterns on an exam, you'll need your own, fully internalized understanding of the deep structure of the course. Law professors sometimes call this "seeing the whole cathedral." The metaphor comes from a famous law review article, Guido Calabresi and A. Douglas Melamed's "Property Rules, Liability Rules, and Inalienability: One View of the Cathedral," which says "this article is meant to be only *one* of Monet's paintings of the Cathedral at Rouen. To understand the Cathedral one must see all of them."[18] (If you want to see what they're talking about, it's easy to find Monet's paintings of the Rouen Cathedral on the web.) You'll need to compose a big-picture view of the course. Each case is just one glimpse. Each case can only be fully understood in light of all the other cases.

So you'll have to pay attention to how your professor connects the cases. Crucially, you'll also have to compose your notes and outline in a way that makes sense of the relationships between the propositions. We'll talk more about that process in part 3. For now, the point is to be aware that you're not just building a list of propositions; you're composing the entire collection of propositions into a much larger system.

The process of editing your notes and creating an outline is a creative process. *You* find the connections between the doctrines. *You* phrase the doctrines in your own words. The cathedral you eventually see will look different from everyone else's.

Fitting the propositions together can be one of the hardest parts of law school. In a class on criminal procedure, I sat through six hours of discussion of when people can resist subpoenas before I realized I had no idea whether we were talking about the Fourth Amendment or the Fifth Amendment. The cases tended not to say, and it hadn't really come up in class discussion. But it mattered a lot. (I won't bore you with the doctrinal trouble I fell into, but it was bad.)

On exams, you'll be able to analyze fact patterns well only if you understand the big picture. So you should often ask yourself, *Why are we talking about this?* Why do we care what the judges decided in this case? How does it fit into the big picture of the course? You'll want to develop the habit of asking yourself why anyone cares about each proposition you encounter.

What does it have to do with the bigger issues the class confronts? If you can answer that question, you're starting to see the whole cathedral.

WHICH PROPOSITIONS SHOULD YOU KEEP?

You cannot possibly retain—in your head or in your notes—every legal proposition you encounter. The most important mental habit a law student can develop is the habit of asking, *Do I need to retain this piece of information? Why?* Challenge each piece of information as if it were an armed stranger knocking on your door in the middle of the night. Why should you let it into your notes? What business does it have there?

It's not easy to know which propositions you should retain. Sometimes you'll hear people asking your professor whether something will be "on the exam." That's the wrong question. Most law school exams give you a set of facts to analyze. So none of the propositions you're learning will be *on* the exam. The legal propositions will appear in your answer. A better question to ask yourself—although it will irritate your professors if you ask it as such—is *might I get credit for mentioning this on the exam?*

When you analyze a fact pattern on a traditional law school exam, you get credit for every relevant proposition you mention and persuasively apply. Even if the professor who wrote the question didn't think it required you to discuss a particular proposition, she might give you credit for it—which would mean the proposition was worth mentioning, and worth studying. When you're distilling the law during the semester, you're looking for the propositions that might get you credit on the exam.

It's not easy to get this right. Maybe something was only mentioned in one of those irritating little casebook "notes" at the end of a long night's reading, and your professor never talked about it in class. Is it worth writing down in your notes?

The bad news: you're going to have to err on the side of learning things. Even if the professor didn't think a particular proposition was important, most exams are graded competitively. The question is if you and your neighbor write the same exam, except that your neighbor cites the little note case and you don't, will the professor give your neighbor an extra point? Often, the answer is yes, even if the note case didn't seem important.

Even so, a great deal of your reading can safely be forgotten, because many of the sentences you read won't be any use to you on the exam. Your job is to retain what you need. Here are a few ideas about how to tell which propositions matter.

Sometimes it's easy to tell which propositions matter, because the author of a case telegraphs what part is most important. The phrase "we hold that" usually means the court is about to tell you what it thinks is the key legal proposition. The same thing is true in class. Whenever a professor begins a sentence with "So the rule is . . . ," you'll hear a great fluttering sound as all of the students in the room start typing at once. Join the flutter—and watch out for subtler clues, because in many cases, it's not so easy. In constitutional law, for example, you will read *Marbury v. Madison*, a gigantic case that contains a boatload of legal propositions.[19] In other classes you'll read cases that seem similarly overloaded with propositions. It will seem hard to know which ones to keep in your notes, and which ones to ignore.

When it's not clear from the case which proposition you're supposed to distill from it, look to the context. You can't know what to retain and what to ignore unless you're seeing the whole cathedral. When you've got the big picture firmly in mind, you'll immediately recognize the propositions that don't fit into it. When you're not seeing the big picture, each proposition looks just as important. So know what chapter you're in. Professors, like casebook editors, think in chapters. When professors plan a syllabus, contrary to what you might imagine, they don't think to themselves, "Here are eight hundred thousand cases I'd like to dump on those little snivelers." They think, "I'd like to explore the concept of criminal intent." Then they put together a chapter on criminal intent, in which each case is supposed to illustrate something about that concept. If you're in the criminal intent chapter, then the relevant propositions in the case are probably those that relate to criminal intent. And you need to understand how the propositions from each case relate to that broader concept.

If you can figure out what you are expected to learn, you can figure out by implication what you don't need to learn. If it's a chapter on criminal intent, then your professor probably doesn't care about the substantive crimes being discussed in that chapter. Maybe one case was murder, one rape, and one burglary. Forget it, except insofar as it's relevant to the criminal intent being discussed.

You can sometimes tell why a professor wants you to read a case by juxtaposing it with other cases you've read. Usually the purpose of putting cases together in a syllabus is to line the cases up so that you can see the differences between them. One case will involve a requirement of premeditation; the next will be similar in a lot of ways, but will involve an exception to the premeditation requirement. The next will involve an alternative requirement. The point will be for you to ask yourself, Why did the courts apply different requirements in these different cases? What is the rule, and what are its exceptions?

Another important source of information about which propositions matter is class discussion. Usually, classes will give you a general idea of what matters and what doesn't. Professors will rarely test you on things that weren't covered in class. It's not that they think it's unfair to test you on things that weren't covered in class; it's just that they tend to use class to talk about the propositions they think are important. Class discussions will show you *why* the professor wanted you to read the case that you read. And what you can safely ignore.

Another way to see what matters is to try to look at your class—the entirety of what you've studied over the semester—as a unified whole. My contracts professor, Robin West, told us that she used to love taking exams. The day you take your exams, she said, is the one day you see the whole structure of the class clearly. It's the day you see the whole cathedral.

(At the time, we all thought she was nuts. But she wasn't. She was telling us what it feels like to *enjoy* thinking about the law. No teacher could ever communicate anything more valuable than that.)

Try to describe the conceptual structure of the class in your mind. How do the chapters relate to each other? Is there a theme that was interwoven throughout the class, like "It's hard to get into federal court"? What units of the class seemed to interest the professor most, and why? If you were going to teach the class, how would you have structured it? Imagine you're explaining what you've learned to a nonlawyer, and see how simply you can phrase it without being inaccurate.

Ask all of these questions with an eye toward applying the concepts you've learned. Do you really understand when the police can search your car and when they can't? Do you understand what factual situations these rules are designed to deal with? The more you play with the concepts, the more they become your own.

The first part of this chapter talked about the broad range of propositions you may have to distill in law school, from black-letter law to theory and social policy. This second part of the chapter focused on how distilling works: rather than just copying down principles from your casebooks, distilling is a matter of restating the law in your own words, applying it, putting it in context, and disregarding the propositions that don't matter. This last part especially gives rise to a concern: what do you miss when you distill a case down to its legal propositions?

What Can't Be Distilled

The distilling method I've just described is a mercenary method. It strips cases down to their bare doctrinal core. I've been telling you to care about concepts only when regurgitating them on exams might get you credit.

That sort of efficiency is key to doing well on exams. But efficiency can also mean missing some vital parts of law school.

Ideally, law school teaches you more than just how to distill and absorb legal propositions. A good law school education develops what Karl Llewellyn called "horse sense": a lawyer's ability to judge good and bad legal arguments the way a trained horse buyer judges horses.[20] It can only be learned by really *experiencing* the cases you study.

Horse sense, as Llewllyn understood it, is not common sense. It's a sophisticated sort of intuition, cultivated by years of practice and experience with other lawyers' views, predictions, and reactions. As chapter 13 will explain, your gut needs training. Horse sense is what helps you predict which arguments will find traction, what consequences will follow from the many decisions you'll make as a lawyer. It can't be boiled down into black-letter propositions.

When you become a lawyer, you'll need to know more than propositions of law, because law isn't just propositions; it's a culture. To be a good lawyer, you'll have to become fluent in its languages. You'll need a feeling for what really persuades people to accept legal propositions. You'll have to understand what kinds of things lawyers agree on and what kinds of things are controversial. Some of the arguments that sound plausible to law students sound hilariously wrong to old judges. Only a practiced gut can tell you why.

As a law student, you read cases, rather than just propositions, because even the legally irrelevant details help you develop a feeling for the culture of the law. You're not just trying to learn the rules; you're trying to learn what *matters* to legislators, judges, lawyers, and clients. To get to the bottom of those shared understandings, you'll have to read between the lines.

The experience of getting immersed in the culture of the law can be pleasurable, although it's not always easy to see this. It's natural to feel as though the law that comes at you so quickly in law school has to be processed in a desperately mechanical kind of way. Just get the propositions down on paper, and move on. You don't stop to admire the nice flinty color of a bullet as it whistles past your ear.

But you'll never be good at law unless you learn to appreciate it. As Anthony Kronman writes, a good lawyer has to be a connoisseur of law.[21] The word "connoisseur" has unfortunately aristocratic connotations, but you see the point: to be good at law, you have to care. If you want to predict how a judge will rule, you have to see the case the way the judge sees it. Most judges want to get it right, whatever "right" means to them. They care. If you don't care much about the law, you won't be able to put yourself in their place and imagine how they'll see your case.

It's like being a wine critic. People respect your judgment about wines because they know you care; they know you spend lots of time on it; they know this stuff is your life. And they're right to respect your judgment for that reason. Kronman writes, "the fact that a person takes special pleasure in an activity is typically (even if not invariably) a condition of acquiring the perceptual acuteness that distinguishes the judgment of a connoisseur from those of others."[22] If you were on trial for your life, you wouldn't want a lawyer who found law boring.

Becoming a connoisseur is just what your professor has in mind for you. Ideally, every student would read every case with deep attention, going far beyond mercenary distilling. In your professor's dreams, when you go home and read a case, you quickly develop a little case brief in your head; you spot the relevant proposition or propositions and faithfully note them down. But then, dreams your professor, you go further.

You turn to the beginning and read again. You stroke your chin. You savor the language, or edit it a little in head. You ask yourself why *this* word and not that one. You ask what other outcomes the court might have chosen. You challenge each step in the logical chain. You weigh the policies. You put yourself in the shoes of the parties as their hopes are shattered or vindicated. You send your mind far ahead along the river of law to see how this opinion shaped its course. You do all this with the first opinion assigned, and then you turn to the next and do it again.

This is how a case should be read. If you really want to understand a case, this is how it must be read. But this is not how you will read most cases. You don't have time. You have too much reading. You're only one person. And it's not really required. Good professors try to design exams that reward deep engagement, but that's not easy to do, and exams often require you just to apply the propositions you've distilled. That means that your classes put heavy pressure on you to focus on the key propositions and ignore everything else.

But don't underestimate your professor's ability to tell from your answers on the exam whether you've given real thought to the questions you've studied over the semester. Genuine curiosity and engagement will show up in your answers, and your professor will look for reasons to give you more points.

And the exams aren't the only reason, or even the best reason, to read deeply. Much of what's great about the law—the things that passionate lawyers find it possible to be passionate about—will not be on your exams.

Lawyers who love their work don't just love the legal doctrines they manipulate; for many of them, it's the people they help, or the policies they
advocate, or the negotiations they navigate, that provide the real satisfactions of law practice. Distilling the law is a fundamental and necessary legal
skill, but when you distill you rub out the details, the human experience—
much of what makes the law matter. So distill ruthlessly, but notice what's
left out.

"I checked it very thoroughly," said the computer, "and that quite definitely is the answer. I think the problem, to be quite honest with you, is that you've never actually known what the question is."

DOUGLAS ADAMS, *The Hitchhiker's Guide to the Galaxy*

5   Issue Spotting

The propositions you've worked hard to distill are not the end product of your work. They're the beginning. They're the sculptor's clay.

A traditional law school exam gives you an imaginary situation and asks you to make legal arguments about it. Before you can make arguments, you have to identify the questions you'll be arguing about. *Issue spotting* is identifying the relevant legal questions presented by a situation, and framing them in the right doctrinal language.

The Right Questions

The first step in issue spotting is noticing the questions that can be asked about a set of facts. The first question—and in law practice, ordinarily the most important question—is exactly what the facts are. Did Mr. Phipps break into the store, or just wander in? Who forged the signature on that balance sheet?

Modern history's most infamous example of issue spotting involved a pure question of fact. Monica Lewinsky had signed an affidavit that said "there is absolutely no sex" between her and President Clinton. In a deposition, Clinton was asked whether that statement was a lie. He spotted the factual issue: Lewinsky had used the present tense ("there *is* absolutely no sex"), and at the time she signed the affidavit she was not having sex with the president. So, in one sense, it was correct to say "there *is* absolutely no sex." But of course Lewinsky's statement could be read more broadly, as a denial of any ongoing sexual relationship. As Clinton explained, "It depends on what the meaning of the word 'is' is." That would certainly have gotten Clinton a point or two on a law school exam. Unfortunately for him, presidential depositions are not graded on a point-score basis.

The challenge on law school exams is usually not to spot purely factual issues like the question about whether Lewinsky lied. (This is *law* school.) Instead, law school will teach you to spot three kinds of issues: issues about which propositions are relevant, issues about how those propositions should be interpreted, and issues about how they should be applied.

FIRST, ASK WHICH PROPOSITIONS ARE RELEVANT

Issue spotting begins with identifying all of the propositions that are relevant to some aspect of the facts in front of you. Say an exam tells you that your client has been charged with bigamy in Texas, and gives you the text of the Texas bigamy statute. The exam then asks you what defenses you might offer on his behalf.

The first step is to collect all of the propositions that might be relevant here—every proposition that might help you attack the bigamy law. You've learned that *a criminal law may not be unduly vague*. The Texas statute says bigamy exists when a married person marries or "purports to marry" a second spouse. So there's an issue: *is the phrase "purports to marry" unconstitutionally vague?*

You've also learned that the Supreme Court struck down a Texas law that prohibited sodomy in a case called *Lawrence v. Texas*.[1] You distilled the holding of *Lawrence* this way: *a state criminal law is unconstitutional if it outlaws consensual sexual conduct*. So that's another issue: *is this law subject to* Lawrence's *prohibition on antisex laws?*

Perhaps you also learned that in 2005, Texas amended its constitution to add this sentence: "This state . . . may not create or recognize any legal status identical or similar to marriage."[2] The amendment was meant to ban same-sex marriages. But after the amendment became part of the constitution, some people noticed a potential problem: isn't marriage itself a "legal status identical to . . . marriage"? If all legal statuses "identical to" marriage are illegal, then marriage itself might be illegal. A number of people, including one candidate for Texas attorney general, argued that Texas had accidentally voided all marriages.[3]

So that's another issue you might need to spot on the exam. Assume your allegedly bigamist client was married only after the 2005 amendment. (It's a good idea to note factual assumptions like these in your answer, because your professor might have been making a different assumption.) If the 2005 amendment really abolished all marriages in Texas, then not only did your client not marry twice—he never married at all. So there's another issue: *are your client's marriages void under the 2005 amendment?*

Now you've spotted three issues, each of which involves a question about whether a certain proposition applies to your case. Some of them relate to the interpretation of legal *texts*. Some of them relate to the interpretation of legal *precedents*. Each of them is a relatively simple issue, because each of them involves only one proposition of law. Exams never stay that simple for long.

Remember, too, that many of the important issues on your exams will involve conflicting propositions—rules that contradict each other. If you've studied two conflicting rules that might apply to the exam's fact pattern, your job on this exam is to identify the conflict of rules. You'll say that two rules might apply, and then make whatever arguments are available under *each rule*. Again, exams don't want the "correct" answer. They want all the possible answers, based on the propositions you've studied in class.

SECOND, ASK WHAT THE PROPOSITIONS MEAN

The second step in issue spotting is to interpret the propositions—to see the questions that might be asked about what they mean. Many propositions can be interpreted in more than one way. For example, you'd get some credit for knowing that *Lawrence v. Texas* struck down a law against sodomy. But on this exam, you'd have to make arguments about exactly how *Lawrence* should be interpreted.

The bigamist will argue that *Lawrence* protects a broad right to enter into intimate relationships, and that this right covers all sorts of things. Justice Scalia's dissent in *Lawrence* warned that "state laws against bigamy, same-sex marriage, adult incest, prostitution, masturbation, adultery, fornication, bestiality, and obscenity" are all "called into question" by the *Lawrence* decision.[4] The prosecutor will argue that Scalia and the bigamist are wrong—*Lawrence* was about private conduct, like sex, not publicly recognized relationships like marriage.

The point here is that the same case can stand for different propositions. Does *Lawrence* mean *citizens have a right to define their own relationships?* Or does it mean *the government must stay out of the bedroom?* You'll need to see the conflict here—and identify both interpretations—to get full credit on an exam. The same is true of the constitutional amendment that may or may not have banned all marriages. It can be interpreted in different ways. You'll need to identify those alternate versions to do well.

THIRD, ASK HOW THE PROPOSITIONS APPLY

Exams also want you to *apply* each proposition to the fact pattern. The fact patterns themselves are often ambiguous. Legal categories don't always map neatly onto the real world, and your professors want you to show that you understand that.

Say you've learned in class that there are two major approaches to the insanity defense. One approach, which is found in the Model Penal Code, recognizes two different ways to show you're insane: either by showing that you can't tell right from wrong, or by showing that you lack the ability to control yourself.[5] But there is another approach, known as the *M'Naghten* rule, under which you can show you're insane *only* by showing that you can't tell right from wrong.[6]

Now let's say your exam uses as its protagonist the character Dr. Impossible from Austin Grossman's novel *Soon I Will Be Invincible*, who (the exam tells you) is on trial for escaping from a top-secret prison. Here's what we know about Dr. Impossible: He is a supervillain who "built a quantum fusion reactor in 1978, and an orbital plasma gun in 1979, and a giant laser-eyed robot in 1984," and who has almost succeeded in conquering the world twelve times. He has been diagnosed with "Malign Hypercognition Disorder." He is literally the smartest man in the world.[7]

Dr. Impossible sometimes seems baffled by his own conduct, wondering, "Why did I freeze the Supreme Court, impersonate the Pope, hold the Moon hostage?" When fighting a superhero, he starts to say, "You won't be laughing when I move the—" and then, stopping himself, wonders, "Why do I always tell people my plans?"[8]

There is evidence that Dr. Impossible became a supervillain by choice. Remembering his origins, he writes, "What do you do when you find out your heart is the wrong kind? You take what you're given, and be the hero you can be. Hero to your own cold, inverted heart." And he remembers the moment he became a supervillain in a way that sounds decidedly intentional: "It was time to stop punishing myself, and start punishing everybody else."[9]

If your exam gave you these facts, you would have to perform two analyses: one under the Model Penal Code, and one under the *M'Naghten* rule. Under *M'Naghten*, can Dr. Impossible argue that he was unable to tell right from wrong? You'll make the best possible arguments on both sides. (This isn't the chapter on argument, but to argue against insanity under *M'Naghten*, you might point out that he knows his heart is "inverted," and that he stops himself from disclosing his plan, which suggests he knows the plan is, in some sense, wrong.)

Then you'll do the same with the Modern Penal Code approach. You've already discussed one of the ways it lets you prove insanity. What about the other: can he argue that he was unable to control himself? (On one hand, he seems to have made a choice to become a supervillain. On the other hand, there is his "malign hypercognition disorder," and the fact that he can hardly stop himself from telling people his plans, and the fact that he's baffled by his own conduct.)

The point here is that you're performing *more than one analysis*. Your answer to this question won't be limited to the IRAC (Issue, Rule, Application, Conclusion) structure that so many people recommend to law students. Instead, for issues like these, you'll identify each proposition that may apply. For each proposition, you'll identify the best arguments on both sides about how it should be interpreted and how it should apply. Then you'll identify the best rebuttal to each of those arguments. So, if we really wanted an acronym, it might be the disturbing IRAACRAAC. As you can see, acronyms aren't all that helpful.

THE SENSE OF WHAT MATTERS

Issue spotting calls on your intuition. You'll need to develop the ability to sense which issues matter and which don't. Sometimes you think you've found a really good question, the kind of question the whole class could talk about for days, but everyone else will think the answer is obvious. (Saying the answer's obvious is another way of saying you haven't spotted much of an issue.) And sometimes when you think the answer is obvious, everyone else will want to argue about it.

Some questions are pregnant with possibility, and others aren't. Learning to see the difference is hard; that's why you spend three years in law school practicing. And you do practice: the questions your professors ask in class are examples of issue spotting, designed to teach you this skill.

Issue spotting can be a creative, inspired process. Different lawyers might "spot" or frame a given issue in very different or even incompatible ways. In fact, what distinguishes really great lawyers is the ability to look at a situation or a doctrinal problem and see the issue in a way that no one else has.

Framing the issue in new ways can be the key to winning a case. One of the best books on legal advocacy, *Making Your Case* by Justice Antonin Scalia and Bryan Garner, advises lawyers to begin every written argument with a statement of the questions presented. Always begin a brief with the questions presented, they say, because framing the case is so often the key to winning it. A great lawyer once said that "he would gladly take either side of any case as long as he could pick the issues."[10]

Issue spotting (or issue framing) is more than just an advocacy skill. It's where you can find the real intellectual rewards of legal thinking. The law of accidents, for example, changed immensely when someone reframed the basic question. Instead of asking whether the defendant *deserves* to bear the cost of the accident, courts and scholars began to ask whether it would have made economic sense for the defendant to take precautions against the accident. (The classic statement of this economic approach is in a famous opinion by Judge Learned Hand, who is the best-named judge in American history, but only because an ancestor of mine named Consider Law never joined the judiciary.[11]) For better or for worse, this kind of reframing—asking questions about economic efficiency, rather than moral deserts—has reshaped American law and legal theory. It's new questions, not new arguments, that really change history.

The issue spotting you'll do as a law student is much easier than the issue spotting you'll do in the real world. (I regret the term "real world"—law school is real!—but it's hard to avoid.) Issue spotting in the real world is hard; it draws on your creativity, your own unique views, and your horse sense. In law practice, it's not unusual for someone to ask despairingly, halfway through a case, "Why didn't we think of *this*?"

Lawyers who are good at issue spotting draw on their experience and intuition. "That reminds me of an issue I ran across once in my admiralty practice. Come to think of it, we may have a similar issue here." Good issue spotting arises from a deeper familiarity with the whole legal system and the patterns that a lawyer has learned to see in it. Like a horse trainer who immediately recognizes worrisome behavior patterns in a young animal, an experienced lawyer sees patterns in a new case that a novice lawyer might miss.

Fortunately, a law student issue spotting on a law school exam doesn't need all that experience, because the world of possible issues on an exam is very small. If you follow the method I suggest in this book, you'll have with you in the exam an outline that lists all of the major topics covered in your class. When it's time to issue spot on the exam, just run down this table of contents as if it were a checklist. Is there a criminal intent issue in these facts? Is there a mootness problem here? Is there a fiduciary duty?

Issue spotting, as we saw above, begins with identifying all of the legal propositions that might be relevant to a given set of facts. In law school, those propositions are limited to what you've covered in class. So your notes and outline contain every possible beginning point for issue spotting. It's just a matter of checking off a list. (If your exam is closed book, you won't have that list with you. But the basic checklist can be short enough to fit in your head.)

Of course, your outline—your checklist of issues—won't get you all the way there. Even if you know what propositions might be relevant to the exam, exam fact patterns are complicated, and issues don't always leap out in bold relief. And you still have to ask whether there are issues about how to interpret the propositions, and how to apply them. Once you've run through your list, there are a few other techniques that tend to work most of the time.

Some Issue-Spotting Shortcuts

Here are a few ways to help point your brain toward the relevant issues—not just on exams, but anywhere you issue spot. This is far from an exhaustive list. Issue spotting is an intuitive process. It has to be learned through practice. But, as with any cognitive skill, experience is much more useful if it's accompanied by *reflection*—by an effort to figure out what works and what doesn't. As you develop your issue-spotting skills, pay attention to what works and what doesn't. These ideas may help get you started.

FOCUS ON WHAT CONFUSES YOU

My high school poetry teacher, Fred Heitkamp, always said that to understand a poem, you have to focus on the part you don't understand. That's true in law too: if something in a legal text confuses you, focus on that. Your confusion probably signals that there's an issue to be explored. Of course, it might just signal a badly written text—but badly written texts are where many interesting arguments start.

Get in touch with the little buzzer in the back of your head that goes off when you're not sure you understand what's in front of you. Learn to listen to that sound, your murk detector, which you'll hear often in law school. It's a friendly sound; it helps you find your way. Ask yourself what confused you. Pinpoint the thing that makes you feel shaky and sit with it until you understand why. You'll have to get comfortable with uncertainty, because it's usually what points you toward the important issues.

AMBIGUITY IS AN ARGUMENT WAITING TO HAPPEN

Confusion often happens when you can imagine two or more different meanings for one word or sentence or paragraph. If you can put your finger on why there are two meanings—or on what those two meanings are—you've identified an issue. For example, consider this wonderfully ambiguous statute from New Jersey, which Eugene Volokh posted on his blog:

> Any person who knowingly has in his possession handcuffs . . . under circumstances not *manifestly appropriate for such lawful uses as handcuffs may have*, is guilty of a disorderly persons offense.[12]

Professor Volokh wrote, "You can guess what my question is." You've spotted the issue here if you can imagine any situation in which reasonable people might disagree about whether someone's possession of handcuffs is "manifestly appropriate for such lawful uses as handcuffs may have."

Be on the lookout for ambiguity in statutory text. If you see statutory language quoted on an exam, it's often because the professor thinks there's an ambiguity you ought to spot.

FOCUS ON WHAT'S NEW

Another way to find an issue is to figure out what's unfamiliar to you. For example, your exams will give you fact patterns you haven't seen in any of the cases you've read. The doctrines you've studied all emerged from particular sets of facts in earlier cases. Your exam will give you a set of facts that fits awkwardly with those earlier sets of facts. Sometimes the first step in issue spotting is asking, *What strikes me funny about these facts?* Ask yourself why your professor wrote the facts this way.

Your professor will introduce new kinds of facts in an exam to illustrate something important about the rules. Say you're studying the constitutional rules about police interrogations. You learn that when a suspect says, "I want a lawyer," the police have to stop asking questions. On the exam, the police resume the questioning without a lawyer present—*three years later*. Is that constitutional? (When this question came up before the US Supreme Court, they decided that the police can start questioning you again after fourteen days. I bet you wouldn't have guessed that on your exam.)[13] The unfamiliar thing here is the time lag. You've never seen a time lag that long. So the question is, does the time lag matter? Now you've spotted the issue.

FOCUS ON YOUR ASSUMPTIONS

An unquestioned assumption is an unspotted issue. So learn to notice your assumptions.

You can often get points on an exam by identifying your assumptions. Say your exam asks this: *does the Constitution allow passage of a law that says only citizens of the United States can be eligible for welfare payments?* You produce a very thoughtful analysis of whether that's constitutional. When you look back at your answer, you realize you've been assuming the law is a state law. That's important, because Congress can do just about anything it wants in the area of immigration; states are a lot more restricted. Suddenly there's a lot more to talk about.

By the way, if you want to make sure you don't miss issues like this, look out for sloppy wording. In the paragraph above, I asked "whether the Constitution allows passage of a law" doing things. *Passage* is a weasel word; as soon as you see it, you should ask, "Who's doing the passing?" Almost any use of the passive voice ("a law may not be passed") creates an issue: who is the subject of that verb? Whenever a sentence fails to make its meaning clear, it creates an issue.

Noticing your assumptions—and the other approaches we've discussed in this chapter—will help you spot a lot of issues, but not all of them will be important. You won't get any credit on the exam for pointing out issues with too tenuous a connection to the rules you've studied and the facts on the exam. The trick is knowing where to draw the line, and that's something you can only learn with practice and reflection. And the best place to practice is on your professors' prior exams, if they're available. Different professors have different expectations about what kinds of issues are worth spotting and discussing on exams. The best way to know what they expect is to look carefully at the old exams, and the sample answers that met their expectations.

They said, when he stood up to speak, stars and stripes came right out in the sky, and once he spoke against a river and made it sink into the ground. They said . . . the trout would jump out of the streams right into his pockets, for they knew it was no use putting up a fight against him; and, when he argued a case, he could turn on the harps of the blessed and the shaking of the earth underground.

STEPHEN VINCENT BENÉT, *The Devil and Daniel Webster*

6   **Argument**

The third skill you'll learn in law school is argument. Once you've spotted an issue, you make arguments about it. *Argument* in this sense doesn't imply a disagreement with anyone. It just means offering your analysis of the questions you found when you were issue spotting. It means *making an argument*, not *getting into an argument*. It means following a chain of legal reasoning through to its end.

The challenge on exams is to identify the best arguments on either side of a question and voice them well. This is important: your job on exams will be to list the arguments *on either side* of the issues you spot. You're supposed to articulate a conclusion. But only after giving the best arguments for both sides.

That's not because there are no right or wrong answers. Students sometimes get the feeling that any answer is as defensible as any other. But some legal arguments are clearly wrong. They're clearly wrong not by virtue of objectively or mathematically provable truths (law doesn't have many of those) but by virtue of deeply shared understandings that make it possible for someone immersed in legal culture to immediately recognize certain arguments as mistaken. Law school trains you to be part of that culture, to share those assumptions, to see which arguments will be immediately rejected by competent lawyers everywhere.

The rest of this chapter will give you an overview of the basic kinds of legal argument. It won't be an exhaustive list. The point is to help you focus on the kinds of arguments you'll be learning to make—the kinds of arguments you'll use on exams—so that you know what to pay attention to and what to practice during the semester.

Law students learn to argue about four basic kinds of things: legal texts; precedents; policy; and facts. When we argue about texts and precedents, we're arguing about *what the relevant legal proposition is.* When we argue about facts, we're arguing about *whether a set of facts falls under a given legal proposition.* Policy arguments can be used for either purpose: to persuade a judge that the legal proposition should be interpreted in a particular way; or to argue about whether a set of facts falls under a given proposition.

Arguments about Texts

Legal arguments often begin with a text. The text might be a constitution, a statute, a regulation, a court rule, or a treaty. It might also be a text created by private parties, like a contract or a will. Each of these texts has authority: someone is arguably required to act in a certain way *because the text says so.* Judicial opinions are texts, too, but leave them aside for now—we'll talk about them in the next section.

Exams will require you to identify the texts that might apply to a set of facts, and then explain the arguments that each side might make about how that text should be interpreted.

When we argue about legal texts in law school, we're arguing about *exactly what legal proposition the text stands for.* In effect, you're arguing about how the legal text should be distilled. So argument requires the skill of seeing the multiple ways a proposition might be construed.

There are no universally accepted rules about how legal texts should be interpreted. Experts on textual interpretation have very different ideas about what kind of arguments about text are proper. And almost everyone thinks that different kinds of texts should be interpreted differently; a constitution is not interpreted the way a contract is.

Although there is no universally accepted general theory of textual interpretation in law, there are some basic forms of argument that lawyers and judges use over and over again. When interpreting a text, lawyers tend to argue about the same basic things: the *text* itself; the *intent* of the drafters; the text's *purpose;* and the *principles of interpretation* that might apply.

THE TEXT ITSELF

The first argument lawyers usually make about legal texts is that the language of the text, or its *plain meaning,* clearly support one interpretation or another. The claim is that the text of the rule unambiguously governs the situation in front of the court.

In law school, the meaning of what you read is rarely plain. You'll spend a great deal of time in law school learning to see multiple meanings in ambiguous legal texts. (By the way: because dealing with ambiguity is such an important skill in law school, reading difficult, ambiguous works of literature may be a great preparation for it. One study suggests that reading Kafka stories significantly heightens one's cognitive ability to recognize patterns in new kinds of information.[1])

You can often create useful arguments by looking at the whole text of a statute or case, rather than just the part you're making arguments about. Say you have a contract that says, "A party to this contract shall be liable for $100,000 in liquidated damages if that party willfully breaches the contract." Your dispute is over what the word "willfully" means. There is another provision in the same contract that says, "This contract shall be governed by the laws of Australia." Now you know that the word "willfully" should be interpreted to mean whatever Australian courts say it means. When you make arguments about the text, don't stop with the particular language that's in dispute.

Even where the text of a rule is plain, nobody thinks that the text should *always* control. For example, the First Amendment says, "Congress shall make no law respecting an establishment of religion." The language could not be more clear: it's *Congress* that is prohibited from establishing a religion. So would it be consistent with the First Amendment for the *president* to issue a proclamation declaring that the United States is an Episcopalian republic and that henceforth all members of our armed forces will take their orders directly from the presiding bishop?

No serious legal thinker believes this, even though the plain text of the First Amendment unambiguously applies only to Congress. We often look beyond the plain text. The question is what other factors we consider, and when, and how much weight we give them in any particular case.

THE INTENT OF THE DRAFTERS

The second kind of argument about text is arguments about the *intent* behind the text: what did the legislators who enacted the statute, or the parties who drafted a contract, or the framers of a constitution, intend that it mean?

Intent arguments are appealing in many ways. When we talk about interpreting a text, we often imagine ourselves trying to understand what the people who created it meant to communicate. When we say, "It wasn't *supposed* to mean such-and-such," we're really talking about intent. Also, focusing on intent seems respectful of the democratic process. The legislators who draft statutes are elected by the people. So judges might want to interpret the statute according to what *they,* not the judges, had in mind.

To understand legislative intent, we often look at legislative history. What did legislators say in their speeches explaining their positions on the law—did they talk about the question presented by your case? Look at the proposals they considered but rejected: do they tell you anything about what the legislators thought the final bill meant?

There are problems with legislative intent; Judge Richard Posner calls the idea of legislative intent "an insult to philosophy,"[2] and Justice Antonin Scalia refuses even to think about what legislators intended.[3] As these and other jurists have pointed out, it's rarely clear exactly what we mean when we talk about a legislature's intent. For example, do we mean the *consequences* that the drafters intended to achieve, or the *principles* they intended to establish? Generally speaking, the framers of the Equal Protection Clause intended to establish the *principle* of equal treatment of all races. But what are the consequences of implementing that principle? Did the framers intend the *consequence* of abolishing segregated schools? (The Senate that passed the Fourteenth Amendment had segregated galleries, and the Congress approved of segregated schools in the District of Columbia.[4]) So is it more consistent with the framers' intent to allow segregation, or to ban it?

Legislative intent arguments are also controversial because they depend on fictions. Because we can't read minds, it's hard enough to know what a single person intended. How could we know what a motley crowd of legislators intended? What does it even mean to talk about what a group of people "intended"? Do we pay attention to the intent of people who voted against the final bill? What about the legislators who voted for the bill just to please a campaign contributor, or those who hated the bill but voted for it to prevent something worse from being enacted?

There are, of course, plausible arguments that might be made on each of these questions; I just wanted to give you a sense of what's at stake. Anyway, even if we could agree on what legislative intent means, there's often no direct evidence of legislative intent, especially in law school classes, where you're usually reading just the materials in your casebook (rather than digging into the *Congressional Record* to see what senators thought about the rule you're studying). In the real world, too, you'll often find that the legislature simply didn't anticipate the question you're grappling with. So we have make other kinds of arguments.

THE PURPOSE OF THE TEXT

Closely related to the question of legislative intent is the question of what *purpose* the text serves. This inquiry focuses not on what actual legislators believed when they voted but on what goals are expressed in the statute. What problem was it meant to solve? Assume that every legal text is designed to accomplish something. To make an argument about purpose, figure out what that purpose was, then claim that your interpretation is more consistent with the purpose.

We know the general purposes of the US Constitution, for example, because they're laid out in the preamble: "to form a more perfect union, establish justice, insure domestic tranquility, provide for the common defense, promote the general welfare, and secure the blessings of liberty to ourselves and our posterity." Unfortunately, when drafters state their goals, they're often pretty vague. How often do you think the language from the preamble actually helps courts figure out the answer to any constitutional case?

Arguments about statutory purpose may seem more palatable than intent arguments. But there are problems with purpose arguments too. Most laws have more than one purpose. In fact, it's often the case that legislators pass laws precisely where there's conflict between different societal needs. The laws are designed to strike a balance between two purposes. In such a case, it will be hard to say that any particular interpretation of an ambiguous provision is consistent with the legislature's "purpose."

Think about environmental laws. In a dispute over whether a manufacturing company is allowed to pollute in a certain way, we could always argue that the purpose of the law was to protect the environment—and, therefore, we should interpret the law in whichever way prevents the most pollution. But the company can usually argue, rightly, that Congress also wanted to limit the burdens on manufacturers. Both sides are right; the law has two purposes that point in opposite directions. Arguments about purpose often fail to make much headway, because legislative purposes are *general*, but the problems courts face are highly *specific*.

PRINCIPLES OF INTERPRETATION

When faced with ambiguity, courts often invoke general principles of interpretation. In the context of statutes and constitutions, there are principles called *canons of construction*—principles or rules of thumb that tell courts in a very general way how to interpret legal texts. For example, there is a canon that says courts should avoid construing a statute in a way that creates a conflict with an earlier statute. There's also the delightfully named *Charming Betsy* canon, under which a statute should not be interpreted to conflict with international law.[5]

These canons of construction are not strict rules; they're guiding principles that judges invoke to explain why they chose one interpretation over another. But the canons of construction are important building blocks in legal argument.

Like the other tools, the canons of construction rarely lead to clear answers. Karl Llewellyn made a list of canons divided into two columns; for each canon, he offered a canon that pointed in the opposite direction.[6] Some people say he was being unfair to canons, and maybe he was.[7] But his basic point is valid: canons of construction aren't *rules*; they're just general guidelines. Judges and lawyers can't apply them mechanically; they have to think about—and argue about—the *reasons* why the canons should apply.

ARGUMENTS THAT THE TEXT DOES NOT APPLY TO YOUR CASE

Finally, even if the language of a text seems to clearly cover your situation, you might be able to argue that the court shouldn't apply it. For one thing, the rule in the text might not apply to your case because its scope is limited geographically. If the rule is an Indonesian law, and your case involves a car accident in Kansas, the rule probably doesn't apply.

The rule also might not apply because some other rule trumps it: the rule might be unconstitutional, or *preempted* by some other rule. Under the Supremacy Clause of the US Constitution, a state law that conflicts with a valid federal law can't be enforced. So remember to ask whether the text in front of you actually applies.

Arguments about Precedents

The second kind of argument lawyers make is arguments about *precedents*. A precedent is something a court did or said in a past case. Usually, when we argue about precedents, we argue about a judicial opinion (in which the court explained why it was doing what it did). When you argue about precedents, you compare the situation in your case with the situation in the earlier case.

Precedents are relevant in all areas of law. Even when the question you're debating has to do with the meaning of a text, precedents are usually important. Legal texts are often too general to give clear guidance about particular cases. To know how the texts apply to any situation, you'll have to look to precedents that interpret those texts.

Not that precedents are always followed. Karl Llewellyn listed sixty-four ways courts deal with precedents.[8] Although the most common way of dealing with a precedent, he found, was simply to cite it and follow it, there are lots of other options, many of which involve creative ways to explain why a particular precedent needn't be followed in the case at hand. I highly recommend Llewellyn's book if you're interested in the nuances of how courts can deal with precedents. For now, we'll stick to the simplest form of the argument, in which one side says *follow the precedent,* and the other side says *don't.*

To make an argument about whether your court should follow a precedent, there are three questions you should ask: (1) Does the earlier court have the power to bind your court? (2) Was the earlier court's statement a holding, or was it dictum? (3) Was the earlier case relevantly similar? These questions all blur into each other, but it's useful to think of them separately.

DOES THE EARLIER COURT HAVE THE POWER TO BIND YOUR COURT?

First: What's the relationship between the two courts? If the earlier case is from the US Supreme Court, and your case is in a lower federal court, then your court can't ignore the precedent; it has to decide whether to follow it or distinguish it. If you're in Kansas state court, and the earlier case is from Ireland, then the earlier case is merely "persuasive authority," meaning it has authority only insofar as it persuades. Your court can agree that the plaintiff would win in Ireland, but decide that in Kansas he loses.

WAS THE PROPOSITION IN THE EARLIER CASE A HOLDING?

Even if the earlier court has the power to bind your court, statements in the earlier court's decision won't all be binding. Courts consider themselves bound only by the *holding* of an earlier case, not by *obiter dicta*— "things said in passing," usually shortened to "dicta" (the plural) or "dictum" (the singular). The holding is the part of the earlier decision that was necessary to the result. The dicta are any other remarks the judge makes about the law.

Say Pete's cement factory explodes, ruining my barn. The court says, "Pete is liable for the damage, because he should have taken better care of his cement factory." That proposition is the holding. The court also says, "If

Pete's cat had snuck into the barn and scratched the walls, Pete would be liable for that too." That proposition is dictum, because the court is talking about something that didn't happen in the situation it was considering.

How do you know a statement is dictum? Imagine the court had made precisely the opposite statement. If the result in the case wouldn't change, it's probably dictum. Or, at least, that's a common argument lawyers make to say something's dictum. In practice, it will often be difficult to decide whether a statement is holding or dictum. In fact, the concept of dictum is somewhat incoherent. As Frederick Schauer observes, what makes statements dicta is that they go beyond facts of their specific cases—but that's also what makes a rule a rule.[9] So courts often have a hard time sorting out whether earlier statements should be described as dicta. Many of the arguments lawyers make about precedent focus on this question.

WAS THE EARLIER CASE RELEVANTLY SIMILAR?

The most common type of argument about precedent is based on reasoning by analogy. Scholars often say that reasoning by analogy is the core of legal reasoning.[10] And this is probably the most common kind of legal argument there is: arguments about whether two cases are similar or different.

Lawrence v. Texas held that a gay couple had a constitutionally protected right not to be criminally punished for having intimate relations—meaning, in that case, sex. Now imagine a lawsuit arguing that a gay couple has a constitutional right to be married. (As of late summer 2012, lawsuits on that question had yet to reach the Supreme Court.) There are similarities and differences between sex and marriage. Both are deeply personal; both involve profoundly important beliefs and feelings about ourselves and our identities. But marriage is (partly) a legal status created by the government. Sex is something people can do without going to City Hall. The question is whether marriage is *relevantly similar* to sex. In other words, should the court treat marriage the same way *Lawrence* treated sex?

You can't know whether the court should apply the same rule to both cases unless you know what similarities matter. So this is what we argue about. One side will say that what mattered in *Lawrence* was that sex is an *intimate* act with powerful implications for one's social identity. So is marriage. The two cases are relevantly similar, so the court should treat them the same.

The other side will say that sex is a *private* act that's none of the government's business. Marriage is a government-created identity. The two cases are relevantly different, so the court should treat them differently. To be convincing, each side will have to come up with an argument about why it is the intimacy of the act, or the privacy of the act, that matters.

WHY READ THE CASE YOUR WAY?

Law school exams will often give you situations in which a court could read the relevant precedents broadly (to cover your case) or narrowly (not to cover your case). Your job is to come up with reasons why the earlier case should be read broadly or narrowly. The lawyer's job is to finish the sentence "Read this case broadly *because* . . ." The world of arguments now opens up to admit almost anything.

You can look at earlier precedents and try to divine from them some theme that cuts in your direction. You can perform a close reading of the earlier decision and try to guess how the earlier court would have preferred to resolve your issue. Or you can make policy arguments: talk about the social consequences that will follow from the establishment of a particular rule, or invoke principles of justice. If you're taking a law school exam, you'll make every reasonable argument you can think of.

Policy Arguments

The third kind of argument you'll learn in law school is the *policy argument.* A policy argument is an argument about what the law *should be.* A policy argument explains why the world will be a better place if the court chooses one interpretation of the law rather than another. Judges are often forced to choose between two reasonable interpretations of the law. When they choose, they can't just give each side a numerical score for persuasiveness and then pick the higher-scoring argument. So when there are reasonable arguments on both sides, judges often want to know which interpretation would be better as a matter of policy.

Lawyers who see policy arguments in judicial opinions sometimes complain about "judicial activism," but everyone wants judges to consider policy in some cases. When lawyers argue that a certain decision would release dangerous prisoners from Guantanamo, or that a judicial decision overrides the will of the majority of citizens, those are policy arguments. To argue that judges should refrain from considering policy arguments because policy is best left to the legislature is, of course, a policy argument.

A good lawyer understands that when the policy behind a doctrine is weak, the doctrine is vulnerable. Courts are more willing to stretch their interpretation of an earlier precedent, or to create exceptions to it, when they are persuaded that the doctrine can't be justified with sound policy.

Judges will often move heaven and earth to avoid an interpretation with consequences they see as dangerous or immoral. An effective legal argument must be supported not only by law, but by a deeper sense that the result sought is the *right* one.

There are several kinds of policy argument that are often seen in law, each of which is based on a different idea of what it means for a decision to be right in this sense. The first kind of policy argument deals with the *consequences* of a given ruling. These arguments involve looking at what will happen *after* the court issues its decision. When a court adopts a rule, people (at least a few) presumably notice, and adjust their behavior. In other words, the creation of a rule gives rise to *incentives*. A good judge thinks about the incentives a ruling would create.

Consider a "three strikes" law under which a person convicted of three felonies gets an automatic life sentence. Say a felon with two convictions on her record robs a house. But there's a witness. Should the robber kill the witness? If the state has no death penalty, and the robber already has two strikes, then the law gives the robber an incentive to kill him. Letting the witness live increases the robber's chances of getting caught. But killing the witness won't lengthen the sentence, because the robber will get the maximum no matter what happens. So the three-strikes law gives the robber an incentive to commit murder.[11]

Unless one of my assumptions was wrong. I said that letting the witness live increases the robber's chances of getting caught, but the robber's chances of getting caught don't depend entirely on the availability of witnesses. The police might devote more resources to catching killers than to catching thieves. Killing someone might draw so much attention from the authorities that the robber is better off letting the witness live.[12]

There's another assumption here that might be questioned: the assumption that robbers decide who to kill based on a meaningful understanding of how the criminal law works. Maybe that's a fantasy: maybe the robber is unlikely to think of any of this, or even to know about the three-strikes law. Then again, maybe not: some laypeople have an extremely sophisticated understanding of the law. For example, as a law review article by Caleb Mason explains, there is a comprehensive overview of Fourth Amendment jurisprudence set forth in the second verse of Jay-Z's song "99 Problems."[13]

To make an argument about incentives, start by asking who will be worried about getting in trouble under the rule. What will their worries make them afraid to do? What will the rule encourage? A rule that forces someone to pay for an injury will create an incentive for similarly situated people to take precautions against that kind of injury in the future. Which is good— unless it's wasteful. We want to make sure that the person taking precautions is the person who can prevent the injury at the lowest cost. (It's much cheaper for the company that makes your car to set up a crash test than for you to do it in your driveway.)

If the court rules for the plaintiff, what will happen to people other than the parties? Will it be a good thing for society? Will the rule be *efficient*—in other words, will it help society achieve its goals without wasting its resources? The school of legal thought called "law and economics" is partly devoted to mapping out the incentives created by legal rules.

Another common kind of argument about consequences has to do with the consequences that a new rule will have for the justice system. These are arguments about the *administrability* of doctrines. Administrability means a number of things: Will courts be able to apply the standard? Will it open the floodgates to a new kind of lawsuit that will overwhelm the courts? Will it be unduly burdensome on other institutional actors, like police officers or local government officials? How workable is the rule?

In 1993, the Supreme Court changed the rules governing expert testimony in a case called *Daubert v. Merrell Dow Pharmaceuticals, Inc.*[14] It sent the *Daubert* case back to the lower courts, instructing them to apply the new standard. Judge Alex Kozinski on the Ninth Circuit was thoroughly annoyed:

> Our responsibility, then, unless we badly misread the Supreme Court's opinion, is to resolve disputes among respected, well-credentialed scientists about matters squarely within their expertise, in areas where there is no scientific consensus as to what is and what is not "good science," and occasionally to reject such expert testimony because it was not "derived by the scientific method." Mindful of our position in the hierarchy of the federal judiciary, we take a deep breath and proceed with this heady task.[15]

Kozinski's point here was *this is a bad rule because courts will have no idea how to apply it.* The rule, he thought, simply wasn't workable.

Closely related to administrability arguments are arguments about *institutional competence*: which institution of government should decide a particular question. Judge Kozinski's complaint about the *Daubert* standard was not just about administrability; it was also about the role of judges. His argument was that *judges are not the best people to make the decision here.*

The issue of institutional competence arises again and again. Arguments about institutional competence claim that the judge is better suited to make a decision than some other body—or that the judge, because of her institutional disadvantages, should step back and let someone else make the decision.

Our legal system often requires one decision maker to defer to another. Appellate courts, for example, usually defer to the findings of trial courts on questions of fact. The appellate courts assume that the trial judges, who saw the witnesses testify, are in a better position to assess the evidence than appellate judges, who only read the transcript. (By the way, this assumption may be wrong. There is now strong scientific evidence that seeing a witness testify in person does not make you better at judging her credibility.[16] But that evidence has yet to precipitate much change in the legal system.) Just as appellate courts defer to trial courts, trial courts often defer to juries on certain questions. Even if a trial judge thinks the jury is wrong, the judge usually lets the jury's verdict stand.

Courts also frequently defer to legislatures. When a judge says to a lawyer, "Isn't the law you're defending a bad one?" the lawyer will often respond, "Maybe, but that's for the legislature to decide." When a Supreme Court justice writes, "The Constitution does not prohibit legislatures from enacting stupid laws,"[17] he is saying that the judiciary should not substitute its judgment for the legislature's—even when it's clear to any reasonable person that the legislature has acted idiotically.

One of the most important kinds of policy arguments is the argument that one outcome or another would be just or unjust. Questions of justice are often part of courts' analysis, and so lawyers need to be ready to answer them. The word "justice" is broad. It can include concepts of morality, fairness, equal treatment, or a thousand other things. Each of those concepts may be relevant to your work in law school. Justice, however it's defined, plays an important role in the work of courts and lawyers.

Sometimes justice is explicitly part of the legal analysis; for example, in many appellate courts, an argument that the parties failed to raise in the court below is waived unless "manifest injustice" would result.

In other cases, justice isn't an explicit part of the legal analysis, but ideas and intuitions about justice play a key role. Consider, for example, the strange case of *Dudley v. Kerwick*.[18] There is a general rule in New York that citizens can't sue to challenge other people's tax exemptions. If your town board decides that your neighbor's property is tax exempt—because, let's say, he starts a church—you lack standing to bring a lawsuit to challenge the decision. That's the general rule, and it's very clear. Or at least it was, until the citizens of Hardenburgh got a bright idea.

In 1977, most of the landowners of Hardenburgh enrolled in the Universal Life Church, an organization which offers instantaneous ordination as a minister to anyone who wants it. Eighty-eight percent of the two hundred people who lived in Hardenburgh signed up as ministers. Among them was the town's tax assessor. The town government gave them all a religious exemption from paying property tax.

James Dudley, one of the few people in the remaining 12 percent, got a call from the tax assessor, who said that if Dudley failed to join the church, he and the other few holdouts would have to pay the full $500,000 it cost to run the town each year. The tax assessor kindly invited him to join the church. He could sign up at the town supervisor's house. Dudley said no.

The New York Court of Appeals had to decide whether to make an exception to the basic rule that citizens can't challenge other people's property tax exemptions. I suspect that you can guess—without knowing anything at all about standing doctrine—what the outcome was. Right: Mr. Dudley's lawsuit was given the green light.

You could analyze this case in terms of incentives. I doubt many economists would see any benefit in allowing a town to coerce a handful of people into paying all of its operating expenses. But there's another way of looking at this, which probably has more to do with what really drove the court: What the town tried to do was ridiculously, preposterously, outrageously *wrong*. Even someone who claims not to care about justice is bound to exclaim, like the nihilist in *The Big Lebowski* whose plan has gone awry, "Iss not fair!"

A good lawyer involved in a case like *Dudley* knows that the court's sense of justice is going to play a big role in its decision. A good legal analysis of any problem includes consideration of the way conflicting ideas about justice or fairness might influence the outcome. Learning to argue well means learning to say intelligent things about justice.

Even though ideas about justice play an important role in many legal cases, students sometimes feel uncomfortable making arguments about justice. They know the professor is going to demand that they support any position they take in class, and it seems hard to support arguments about justice. Who's to say something is unjust?

And there is pervasive idea out there that real lawyers don't care about justice. Felix Frankfurter once said to Oliver Wendell Holmes, who was on his way to work at the Supreme Court, "Do justice, sir, do justice." Holmes replied, "That is not my job. My job is to play the game according to the rules."[19] Lawyers sometimes get very excited about this quote. But Holmes also said, "The law can ask no better justification than the deepest instincts of man."[20] Some of those instincts have to do with justice.

Lawyers work in the *justice* system; we can't afford to be ignorant of intuitions about justice, and we need to know how to make arguments about it. Nor is it possible to keep justice out of doctrinal analysis. When a judge says your appeal is going to be dismissed unless you can show "manifest injustice," you'd better be aware that the word "injustice" may have specific meanings, defined by case law, and that those meanings may differ from your gut instincts in key ways. But you'd also better realize that the judge you're addressing is a human being who also has gut instincts about justice. And when the judge asks you, "Please explain: what's the injustice here?" you'd better not say, "That is not my job."

Even if terms like "justice," "fairness," and "morality" are often broad and vague, sometimes our sense of justice does give us clear answers. Justice isn't just a matter of idiosyncratic personal preferences. On the contrary, it's often a simple matter on which virtually everyone agrees. Say you're a tax lawyer, and you're trying to persuade a court to interpret some tax law in a new way—a way that would spare your client (and, in the future, everyone else) from paying a particular penalty. What about all the people who've paid that penalty in the past? The unfairness here may be tolerable, or not, but few lawyers would deny that it exists. If you fail to anticipate a concern like this, your client may suffer.

Some justice arguments are built not on personal intuitions, but on well-established principles that are embedded in our legal system. One of these is the principle of consistency, the idea that courts should be treating like cases alike. Another is this: "The law holds," Blackstone wrote, "that it is better that ten guilty persons escape than that one innocent suffer."[21] You can frame a good policy argument around that famous proposition without ever drawing on your own personal conceptions of justice. You're talking about the *system's* understanding of justice, rather than just your own.

Not that there's anything wrong with your personal intuitions. On the contrary, they're a vital source of information about any decision. The challenge is framing them in terms of legal doctrine and broadly accepted norms. Your intuitions about justice often give you a starting point from which you can make intelligent arguments about what's fair and what's right.

Analogies can make this easy. There are some things that everyone agrees are unfair. If you have troubling articulating why something seems unjust to you, try making analogies to things we all agree on. For example, if you're debating the death penalty, make an analogy to torture. If we can assume there's a consensus among legal authorities that torture is intolerable (can we?), then you can argue against the death penalty by saying execution is similar to torture.

You'll often get credit for discussions of justice or fairness on an exam if you use them in the right context. But pay attention to your professor. Some professors frown on discussions of justice in the classroom. How is that possible, when legal reasoning is so inextricably bound up with debates about morality, and when the concept of justice is so frequently part of substantive legal analysis? There is a saying: "If you . . . can think about a thing that is inextricably attached to something else without thinking of the thing which it is attached to, then you have a legal mind."[22]

If you notice that arguments about justice or morality are always dismissed in a given class because your professor is a hardcore economist who only wants to talk about incentives, it probably won't pay to talk about justice on the exam. But that doesn't mean you shouldn't think about it.

Although arguments about justice are important, it would be dangerous to assume, as some students do, that judges ignore the law and simply decide cases on the basis of their personal intuitions and preferences. Lawyers who believe this caricature frequently make fools of themselves in oral arguments. They think judges are just politicians in robes. As a result, they're unable even to speak the same language as the judges. Sometimes intuitions don't prevail. And one of the most important things you'll learn in law school is to treat your intuitions about justice as *just one* of the factors that need to be analyzed when you're thinking about a case. Justice matters; but it's important to see how it matters.

You need to make a distinction between *intuitions* about what's right and *legal arguments* about justice. Arguments about justice often make the difference between winning a case and losing it. Intuitions about justice matter, and good lawyers work hard to understand them. But if intuitions can't be formulated into cogent legal arguments, they're an unreliable predictor of legal outcomes.

Consider the case of *United States v. Van Meerbeke*.[23] The defendant was accused of masterminding a scheme to smuggle opium into the country. The prosecution's main witness was Reuben Fife, who had met the defendant in the Haight-Ashbury district of San Francisco during the Summer of Love. The two became friends, and eventually decided to smuggle some opium in from India. Fife was supposed to bring the opium to London in a false-bottomed suitcase, where he was to swap suitcases with a coconspirator. But the coconspirator, nervously lurking around the airport, caught the eye of airport security, and both of them were arrested. Fife pled guilty, and agreed to testify against Van Meerbeke, who'd masterminded the whole scheme.

At the trial, the false-bottomed suitcase was part of the evidence, and the prosecutor asked Fife to explain to the jury how it worked. As Fife was demonstrating the uses of the false bottom, he noticed a small chip of opium still stuck in the suitcase. He did the only thing a self-respecting hippie drug smuggler could do: he grabbed it and swallowed it.

The trial judge noticed Reuben Fife swallowing the opium, but—for reasons that are lost to history—didn't say anything. Four days later, Fife was back on the stand. He noticed that some chips of opium had fallen out of the suitcase and were still sitting on the floor of the witness stand. Naturally, he ate those too. But this time, the defense attorney saw him. When the attorney asked him about it during cross-examination, Fife—who had taken LSD more than three hundred times in his life—admitted eating the opium, but denied that it had affected his testimony. He said that the chips had given him only "[m]inor hallucinations, the kind that happen to me sometimes when I don't take drugs."

The defense moved for a mistrial or to strike Fife's testimony. The trial judge denied the motion. You can see, can't you, why a mistrial might seem intuitively appealing here? Something is wrong with a trial in which the government's star witness is snacking on opium chips and hallucinating during his testimony. It's *not fair* to send someone to jail when his trial was a bizarre circus.

The Second Circuit shared that intuition, and its opinion is permeated with a kind of shocked disbelief. But the court concluded that nothing in the law required the trial judge to declare a mistrial. There just wasn't a good legal argument lining up with the intuition. If anything, the defendants benefitted from the chance to tell the jury that the government's star witness was a drug-addled maniac. So, despite the absurd breach of decorum, the verdict stood.

We have to learn to translate our intuitions about fairness and justice into cogent legal arguments. The conduct of the *Van Meerbeke* trial was shocking (or at least very, very funny), but shock alone doesn't win lawsuits unless the lawyers can fit it into the right doctrinal boxes. Justice can be an important factor in legal analysis; sometimes it's the most important factor. But if justice is no more than an intuition or a gauzy sense of what feels right, it may make no difference at all.

That's why law professors delight in giving you cases where the result feels wrong. They're trying to teach you that law is more than just feelings. Just don't get the idea that lawyers are supposed to be androids with cold, dead hearts. Law can't be separated from intuitions about justice, or from feelings in general. It's a human activity. Becoming a lawyer means developing a sense of when ideas about justice and fairness make a difference, and why.

Arguments about Facts

A final category of argument that you'll learn is arguments about facts. Every traditional exam will require you to apply the propositions you've learned to facts. You'll be asked to make arguments about which legal category a given set of facts falls into. So it's crucial that you pay attention, in class and in the reading, to arguments about how to categorize facts.

In traditional classes, you'll rarely have an argument about what the facts *are.* Here's a question your exam won't ask: "Gina says that her employer's real reason for firing her was her race. The employer denies it. Who's telling the truth?" Of course, questions like these are an extremely important part of many lawyers' practice. But traditional classes deal with facts in casebooks, not facts in the world.

Usually, exams ask you to apply legal propositions (the ones you worked so hard to distill) to a given set of facts. Your challenge will be to make arguments about which legal category the facts fall into—like whether a particular act of sloppy driving falls into the category of "negligence" or the category of "recklessness." We call these arguments problems of *application of law to fact.*

A judge once said that "the state of a man's mind is as much a fact as the state of his digestion."[24] But the legal terms we use to categorize that state of mind aren't facts at all. We create legal categories like "depraved indifference" and "probable cause" to make sense of an undifferentiated world. When a judge decides whether a killer acted with "depraved indifference," it's not as if depraved indifference is a thing that has an empirical existence. It's an *interpretation* of the facts. As Judge Posner writes, the law's challenge is to make "dichotomous cuts in continuous phenomena."[25] Your exams won't ask you to *find* facts—to go out in the world and find out what really happened or how things really are. But exams will ask you to make arguments about how a given set of facts should be interpreted.

Here's an example of an argument about how to categorize a set of facts. In 2002, the justices of the Supreme Court disagreed about whether a school district in Oklahoma could require drug tests for students in nonathletic student groups.[26] The Fourth Amendment requires that any search be "reasonable," and drug tests are searches. The drug tests weren't reasonable if drugs posed no real threat. To decide whether the tests were reasonable, the Court had to decide how bad the drug problem was among the students in nonathletic clubs.

Lawyers defending the school's policy argued that members of a high school band "perform extremely precise routines with heavy equipment and instruments in close proximity to other students." Also, they observed that members of Future Farmers of America "are required to individually control and restrain animals as large as 1500 pounds." The federal government, supporting the drug tests, warned that members of Future Homemakers of America may handle "cutlery or other sharp instruments."[27]

Justice Ginsburg doubted that these hazards were enough to give the school reason to drug test these particular groups of students:

> Notwithstanding nightmarish images of out-of-control flatware, livestock run amok, and colliding tubas disturbing the peace and quiet of Tecumseh, the great majority of students the School District seeks to test in truth are engaged in activities that are not safety sensitive to an unusual degree.[28]

But she was in the minority. Justice Thomas, for the majority, found the dangers real enough, and upheld the searches. They were looking at the same factual record, but disagreeing about which legal category it fell into.

Another kind of factual argument has to do with what will happen in the real world after the court reaches its decision. There's a big overlap between policy arguments and arguments about the factual consequences of legal rulings. Judges sometimes make unfounded assumptions about the factual consequences of their decisions, as Oliver Wendell Holmes noted when he wondered, "What have we better than a blind guess to show that the criminal law in its present form does more good than harm? . . . Does punishment deter?"[29]

One remarkable example of unfounded assumptions about the consequences of a decision came when the Supreme Court had to decide in *Clinton v. Jones* whether to allow someone to sue the US president during his presidency. President Clinton argued that the lawsuit should be postponed until he was out of office; he argued that the decision would have bad factual consequences—distracting the president from his job. The Supreme Court unanimously rejected that argument, saying that the case "appears to us highly unlikely to occupy any substantial amount of [the president]'s time."[30] That particular lawsuit, of course, led to the Lewinsky investigation and Clinton's impeachment. Whether you think that whole business was a good idea or not, nobody thinks the Court was right about how much of the president's time it would take up.

Some factual assumptions are hard to test. Our adversary system of justice is based on the idea that we get the best outcome when we allow two partisan attorneys to argue forcefully each side of a case. The idea is that the truth will emerge from this conflict. This probably isn't an unreasonable assumption, as assumptions go. Our adversarial process, in which an attorney tries to refute each claim the other attorney makes, has been compared to the scientific method, in which scientists advance a hypothesis and then try to refute it. But David Luban notes that a scientist, unlike a trial lawyer, "does not proceed by advancing conjectures that the scientist knows to be false and then using procedural rules to exclude probative evidence."[31] Our assumptions might reasonably be questioned.

Increasingly, legal scholars are trying to pay attention to other fields of inquiry that can give us valuable information about the way legal decisions will affect the world. Economics, psychology, sociology, and other sciences are having an increasingly powerful impact on legal thinking. For your purposes, it's important just to be aware that it's often possible to question the factual assumptions behind policy arguments. And questioning assumptions can often get you points on exams.

Another important category of factual arguments involves how facts should be handled. Rules of *evidence* are designed to make sure our judicial system takes account of certain facts, but not others. In a criminal trial for shoplifting, the prosecutor would not be allowed to offer evidence that the defendant was a communist, because that's not the kind of fact that juries ought to be considering. Many evidentiary arguments have to do with whether juries can be trusted with a particular piece of information. (In that sense, many evidentiary arguments are arguments about institutional competence.) Others involve *burdens of proof* and *presumptions*. Sometimes courts have to reach a conclusion when there's no evidence for either side. In those situations, the arguments will center on who has the *burden of proof*. The party with the burden of proof is the party that loses if there's no evidence. If there is no evidence on a question, courts may use *presumptions*—meaning they assume something to be true unless there is evidence to the contrary. If a lawyer has no evidence on her side, she might argue that the other side has the burden of proof, or that the court should adopt a presumption. These are arguments about how the court should handle a *lack* of facts. And lack of facts is often the biggest problem in a given case.

What's Good about Good Arguments?

Some law students feel troubled by the way law school asks them to argue both sides of any question. This is what many people say they hate about lawyers: we're two-faced; we manipulate the truth; we turn up into down and bad into good. Is your integrity threatened when you learn to argue both sides of any question? Should a decent person want to acquire this skill?

Legal ethicists have long struggled with whether decent people should want to work in a profession where "they are required by their duty of zealous advocacy to present colorable versions of the facts that they do not themselves believe and to make colorable legal arguments that they reject."[32] What's the difference between lawyerliness and hypocrisy?

It's important to separate two questions: whether you want to work in a job that requires you to say things you don't believe, and whether you want to learn to see things from both sides. The job question comes later. (By the way, there are plenty of legal jobs that will rarely require duplicity, from in-house counsel positions to certain kinds of public interest and government work.) The second question—whether it's a good thing to learn, in law school, to see both sides of a question—must be answered, resoundingly, yes.

Even the most honest lawyers need to be able to make arguments on both sides of an issue. If you have an adversary, you need to anticipate what they might say. Even if you don't have an adversary, the best way to test your ideas is to imagine an argument against them. A lawyer writing a law review article, for example, might ask, "What's the best argument that I'm wrong?" Being good at argument means being agile; it needn't mean sacrificing integrity.

One of the core purposes of a liberal education is to teach what Martha Nussbaum calls "narrative imagination": the ability to put yourself in others' shoes, to imagine, although not uncritically, what it's like to be different than you are.[33] Empathy and imagination are just what legal argument requires. The secret to arguing well is not disregarding your own beliefs, but taking full account of someone else's—an imaginary person who believes the argument you need to make. Don't be afraid to see things from another person's point of view, to let their arguments come out of your mouth.

As you develop the skill of legal argument, your professional personality begins to emerge. Learning to argue involves making a million tiny decisions that have a profound effect on what kind of lawyer you're going to be: not just how relentlessly you'll push your client's positions, but what kind of voice you'll use when you do it. What's your style? What does your professional voice sound like? Are you funny? Somber? Surprising? Dead-eyed? What does it feel like to make a good argument?

Here are two ways of describing the feeling of argument:

> But I do remember that incredible surge of power and satisfaction I felt when I made a strong argument and dragged people over to my side of the question.[34]

> It is inherently beautiful to follow one's professional code, as a monk follows the rule of his order. Like an elegant solution in mathematics or a position in chess, a contract may be beautiful because it successfully balances and satisfies competing tensions. . . . In like manner, a lawyer's brief can be satisfying through the beauty of its organized logic.[35]

What feels good about argument: the surge of power, or the monkish pleasure of craft? Your answer, the answer you build slowly, over your lifetime, defines you. James Boyd White writes, "At the end of thirty years you will be able to look at shelves of briefs, think back on negotiations and arguments and interviews, and say, 'Here is what I have found it possible to say.'"[36] Every lawyer makes arguments about the law (what I'm calling "argument" includes the whole range of analytical law talk). Your identity as a lawyer will be defined in part by the way you make yours. Law school is your chance to experiment.

And if law school is fun for you (it is for some people), it's probably because you love to argue, to talk a chain of legal reasoning through to its end. There's nothing that quite compares with the moment when an argument suddenly works, when you feel a pleasurable click somewhere in the brain and know just what to say.

Need I explain, in passing, that there is nothing in the cow's anatomy that requires milking her at the ungodly hours chosen by most farmers?

HENRY TETLOW, *We Farm for A Hobby—And Make It Pay*

PART III

The Work You'll Do

Part 2 explained the three skills that law school exams require. This part of the book explains how those skills are developed and deployed during the semester. It covers the work law students do during the semester: reading, class discussion, notes, outlines, study groups, and law review. Each chapter will help you understand the purpose of the different kinds of work: what you can gain from them, and how they relate to the exams on which you're judged.

Each chapter also suggests a method, a way to approach the work, and this is where I get nervous. I said earlier that I wanted to show you what choices you'll be making in law school, rather than telling you which answers are best, and I meant it. But I can't explain how note taking and outlining work without giving you examples, and the examples I give may as well be good ones. So this part of the book is going to give you specific suggestions. But please: Do not follow them like rules. Instead, use this part of the book as a starting point for your experiments with different ways of studying. As you work, pause every once in a while to ask yourself how the work you're doing bears on your ultimate goal. Trust your instincts: if you feel like you're wasting time, you probably are. But don't just rely on your instincts. Give some thought to the process.

Experiment fearlessly with different approaches to managing your work. If an outline isn't going to help you on the exam, don't outline. If reading before class isn't helpful, try reading after class instead. Do whatever helps you process the information most efficiently, whether it's what your colleagues are doing or not.

Don't be afraid to make the wrong decision. Your choices about how to use your time may not be the most efficient or smartest. At the beginning, you can be sure they won't be. But that's the point of learning: you get better, which means you look back at what you used to do, and it looks worse. Besides, in law school you're competitively graded. Everyone else is learning too. You don't have to get it right the first time.

I called up Toni Morrison and I said, "Do people tell you they have to keep going over the words sometimes?" and she said, "That, my dear, is called reading."

7   Reading

Distilling your reading is difficult for a number of reasons. For one thing, the law suffers from what Bryan Garner calls "a history of wretched writing, a history that reinforces itself every time we open the lawbooks."[1] It isn't always wretched—occasionally, judicial writing is gorgeous. But you'll still encounter opinions that start with sentences like this: "A number of grounds are assigned for reversal." What does "assigned" mean? Who's doing the assigning? Reversal of what, and by whom? You'll have to waste lots of nights answering questions like these.

Even when the writing is good, it's hard to understand. When you learn the law, you start in the middle. American law develops case by case, over hundreds of years, with each case building on a long chain of other cases. You can't start at the beginning. Reading case law is like entering a conversation that started a long time ago and trying to pretend you know what everybody is talking about.

It would be easier if we didn't have to start in the middle. It's tempting to get the law from treatises, study guides, or commercial outlines: legal materials that simply tell you what the law is, instead of making you distill it down from a mess of rambling judicial gobbledygook. But practicing lawyers have to be able to read and distill cases, because practicing lawyers always start in the middle. Each case they handle takes place against a background of hundreds of past cases. The lawyer's job is to situate today's case in the middle of all those past cases. Even if you have a treatise that happens to discuss your issue, you can't trust that it's up to date—you have to look up the cases yourself, to see where the law is. And cases don't begin with a book setting out the black-letter principles that govern your case; instead, they begin with a client who walks in and demands to know whether he can sue his mom.

So you have to be able to figure out the black-letter principles for yourself. Once you learn how to find the important bits, it won't feel nearly as strange.

Where the Propositions Are

When you read a case, your job is to identify the relevant legal propositions it contains. As chapter 4 explained, a proposition is relevant, for your purposes, if it is likely to be useful to you on the exam.

Many of the cases you read will contain only one legal proposition that you'll need to remember. For example, *Rylands v. Fletcher* stands for the proposition that people who engage in inherently dangerous activities are liable for harm they cause to others, no matter how careful they were.[2] If you study *Rylands,* that's probably the only thing you'll need to know about it.

On the other hand, *Marbury v. Madison* contains more than a dozen propositions that my constitutional law professor considered relevant.[3] We spent three weeks discussing it. If your professor sees twelve relevant legal propositions in a case, you'll need to see all twelve too. And if your professor thinks a case embodies an important proposition about how judges should decide cases—like *Do not antagonize the executive branch unless absolutely necessary*—then you'll want to write down that proposition too.

Remember: your units of thought are legal propositions, not cases. If a case represents more than one relevant proposition, give each proposition its own entry in your notes and its own space in your head.

Some cases will contain discussions of earlier cases. Sometimes those earlier cases don't appear in your casebook. To understand the rules you're talking about, you have to know what propositions those earlier cases stood for. This can be maddening: it may look like you're only assigned to read one case, but in fact you're responsible for knowing the propositions from three.

Then there's the material between the cases. Many casebooks contain little "Notes" written by the editors, which contain summaries of other cases that delve more deeply into the principles discussed in the cases you've read. Unfortunately, you may need to remember propositions from them too. A Note packed with propositions means more work for you—if those propositions have the potential to earn points on exams.

Sadly, most professors don't understand that reading takes longer if it contains proposition-filled Notes. In most courses, you will be assigned something like thirty pages of reading a night, as if pages were a relevant measure of how long reading takes you. Pages have nothing to do with it. It's the density of propositions that determines how long the reading will take.

The Skills Reading Teaches

The first skill you'll develop through reading cases is distilling the law—it's the only way to get through them. A case contains a lot more than just the propositions you'll want to save for the exam. Sorting through all the material in a case will get easier with practice, but at first you'll want to use a sort of crutch called a *brief* to help find your way.

Briefing cases is the practice of summarizing a case by tersely identifying its facts, its holding, and the reasons for the holding. The conventional wisdom is that briefing cases to prepare for class is something first-year law students should do for a few weeks in the beginning, and then stop. The conventional wisdom is right.

If you do a quick Google search, you'll find lots of suggestions for what goes into a case brief. Some lists are very short, like mine (facts, holding, reasons). Others are very long, and include things like procedural history, description of the parties, and so on. Be careful. If you're in a class on torts or contracts, you probably don't care much about the procedural details of the case. Early on, you might want to practice sorting through all of those aspects of each case, just to get familiar with them. But as you go on, you'll want less detail, because you won't need it.

You will soon wean yourself off case briefs. After a few weeks of reading cases, you'll stop seeing dense legal discussion and start seeing propositions of law. Once you've taught yourself to see the separate elements of each case, there's no need to keep briefing. Just write down what you think you'll need to retain: the relevant propositions, and enough of the facts and the reasoning to let you understand them when you look back at your notes later. As you get deeper into law school, you'll get better at seeing the relevant propositions in each case. That's all you need in your notes. The rest is just context.

Some students get their case briefs from books, rather than briefing the cases themselves. You'll find your law school bookstore full of books designed to help law students with specific classes; while some offer general outlines of subject areas like torts and contracts, others are keyed to specific casebooks and contain brief summaries of the facts, holding, and reasoning of each case you read. In general, there's nothing wrong with referring to books that try to summarize the law you're studying—they can be helpful, although there's always a risk that the author of those books understands the law differently from your professor. And you might find a guide written by your professor, or written by the author of your casebook, which could help you figure out what the casebook means in some of the more cryptic discussions. If used sparingly, the right study guide can save you time that might be better spent elsewhere. But be wary of books that offer you canned case briefs. Relying on someone else's case briefs is like paying someone to learn to ride a bicycle for you. The point of briefing the cases you read is to learn to distill the law yourself. You won't learn how to distill cases if someone else does it for you.

The second skill you'll develop through reading is issue spotting. In every case you read, the court identifies what it believes are the relevant issues in the case. You'll learn to be critical of the issue spotting you see. What other issues might the court have chosen to address?

Issue spotting is also the point of some of the little Notes that appear after cases in your casebooks. The Notes will sometimes give you a series of questions that you couldn't possibly answer, like "Would the rule of this case also apply if the victim were a cat?" or "If good faith is really a defense to fraud, which party should have the burden of proof on this issue?" You may feel like screaming, "How should I know?" at whoever wrote the Notes. That's because you're used to reading questions that are designed to be answered.

The questions in your casebook's Notes are examples of issue spotting. Your casebook is showing you some of the questions that might be asked about a case. Your instinct is to try to answer the questions, but that's not your job here. It might be good practice, but the *questions* have value in themselves. Ask yourself whether they're good questions. If they didn't occur to you while you were reading the case, ask why not. You might even try inventing arguments to answer the questions, just to see what they might look like. But noticing questions is itself a critical skill.

Finally, your reading is also an opportunity to practice argument. You want to develop the habit of imagining the argument against whatever you're reading. Challenge what you read. Remind yourself to disagree with the holdings of cases on a regular basis. Train yourself to finish the sentence "That's clearly wrong, because—" This isn't just a good way to develop your argument skills; sometimes lively skepticism is the only way to keep yourself awake.

Study Guides and Other Outside Reading

I mentioned commercial case briefs earlier; now a quick word on the commercial outlines, Nutshells, treatises, and the myriad other study aids into which law students pour their money. Some of these will help you identify and understand the relevant legal propositions. Others won't.

Other students may tell you that you need study guides; your professors may tell you not to use them. Or vice versa. Be skeptical. Your colleagues haven't taken the exam yet, so they don't know any more than you do. As for your professor, it's been many years since she had to approach this course from the perspective of someone who knows nothing. Nor has she had to take her own exam. So she doesn't necessarily know what will help you prepare for it.

And that, of course, is the trick: to use study guides insofar as they will help you prepare for your professor's exam. Before you dive into a study guide, you should know *why* you're diving in.

One good reason to look at a study guide is when you're feeling uncertain about a particular legal issue. Your professor talks about "compensatory damages," and so does your casebook, but nobody stops to tell you what the phrase actually means. Great! A treatise can probably give you a good concise explanation of what makes compensatory damages compensatory.

Commercial study guides can also help show you the big picture of the law. The Nutshell series, for example, will give you very short chapters summarizing the major concepts in each class. It can be helpful to step back and see, for example, that all of those cases you've been reading in your first few weeks of Contracts are just talking about what it takes for the law to decide that two people have made a binding agreement.

The problem with any outside reading—aside from the fact that it takes time, which you haven't got much of—is that its author has no idea what your professor thinks the law is, or what aspects of it she finds important. (Unless your professor is the author of the study guide, in which case it's worth more attention.) If you're looking for an explanation of what your professor is talking about when she says "assumption of the risk," a treatise or study guide can help. But be careful: your professor may understand it differently than your study guide.

You've got enough to read. If you look at outside sources, have a good reason. But then, that should be your approach to everything.

If You're Falling Behind

If you fall behind on the reading, you have choices to make. Here's what you *shouldn't* do: race your eyes across two hundred pages of reading in two hours. You don't get any points for having seen every assigned page. You get points on the exam for being able to identify and apply the legal propositions that are waiting to be distilled in each case. So the question is how much time you can commit to catching up, and what strategy will make the most of that time.

If you're severely behind—you missed half the course, and it's the week before exams—you should probably go straight to the commercial outlines or study guides and just lift the propositions straight from their case summaries. Your understanding of the propositions will be thin, and it'll be difficult to apply them. But if you have to strip your semester's work down to its core, focus on just getting hold of the propositions by any means necessary.

If you're moderately behind—you missed a week's reading—then there are a number of strategies that might work. Remember, the point is to get the most important propositions into your notes in distilled form, so that you can apply them on the exam. So start by figuring out which are the most important propositions. Get a classmate's notes, if you can, and see which cases your professor emphasized in class.

Read those core cases if you can; steal summaries from commercial outlines if you can't. Skip cases that weren't discussed in class. Ignore extra material like Notes in your casebook. Again, the point is to focus on the main propositions themselves. If you do nothing else, try to make sure the most important propositions are available in your notes.

Socrates, even before I met you they told me that in plain truth you
are a perplexed man yourself and reduce others to perplexity. At this
moment I feel you are exercising magic and witchcraft upon me and
positively laying me under your spell until I am just a mass of helpless-
ness. . . . My mind and my lips are literally numb, and I have nothing to
reply to you.

MENO, after being questioned by Socrates, in Plato's *Meno*

8 Speaking in Class

The more you understand about how the Socratic method is supposed to
work, the more you'll be able to get out of class discussion. So this chapter tries to explain what can be gained from speaking in class, and how to
get the most out of it. It will also talk about bad professors: what they do,
how to protect yourself, and how to have a good experience in spite of
them.

Class participation is usually not graded. When you speak in class, your
performance has very little direct impact on your grade. Although many
professors give some credit for class discussion, it's a tiny part of your overall grade. It's very important to remember this if you're feeling nervous
about being called on.

But that's not to say that classes don't matter. Even though you may not
get credit for speaking in class, there's much to be gained there. When the
professor orchestrates a class well, students who take part in the conversation are richly rewarded. There's a lot of fear and resentment about the
Socratic method, and sometimes it's justified. But there are also some very
good reasons to speak.

Seven Reasons to Speak in Class

To understand the reasons for speaking in class, it's important not to get
the wrong idea about what law school classes are like. When we talk about
the Socratic method, we're talking about a whole palette of teaching techniques, including

- calling on students randomly and without warning;
- keeping one student on the spot for a long time;
- making students recite the facts of a case in detail;
- asking an endless series of questions without giving answers;
- probing the students' answers for inconsistencies and unexamined assumptions.

The Socratic method is also a mood. When you think of the Socratic method, you might picture a professor who is cold and impersonal, a model of precision and heartless rationality. That professor is the scariest thing about law school. But this is a caricature, not a picture of your actual law professor.

It's unlikely you'll ever see a professor who uses all of the classic Socratic techniques. As Phillip Areeda wrote, "The relentless questioner who never utters a declarative sentence is extinct."[1] Although most professors use a question-and-answer format at least some of the time, studies suggest that the Socratic method these days is usually used in a modified, softer form: professors let students know in advance when they'll be called on, or rely on volunteers, or let students pass on answering questions.[2]

That's not to say that speaking in class is easy. It's stressful and challenging, and sometimes painful. In badly run classes, it can even be damaging. But it's hard for students to know whether their stress is a product of genuinely bad teaching or just a product of culture shock. Even in a well-run class, the stress can make it easy to lose sight of what's good about the experience of speaking. So here are some things you can hope to get out of a good class.

1. GET BETTER AT LEGAL REASONING

First, speaking in class can help you get better at legal reasoning. Being questioned about the cases you've studied forces your brain to attack them in new ways. If your professor is skillful, she'll guide you to insights you wouldn't have been able to reach on your own. It matters immensely that these insights come from you. It's like the difference between dissecting a cadaver yourself and watching someone else do it.

2. LEARN THE LIMITS OF LEGAL REASONING

Speaking in class is frustrating, because the professor's questions never end. She'll ask you why a case should come out a certain way, and you'll answer with a principle—and then she'll show you that your principle leads to absurd conclusions in some situations. She'll ask you questions that expose the assumptions underlying your argument, and show you that the assumptions you're making are ultimately hard to justify.

That's because all principles lead to absurd conclusions in some situations, and all arguments ultimately rest on assumptions that are hard to justify. Legal reasoning, like all reasoning, has limits. There is no grand theory of law that can explain all cases, and there's no principle that doesn't sometimes lead to bad results. That's one of the key things you learn from class discussion. Assert any principle, and your professor will ask questions that take you further and further into confusion. But the lesson you should take from this is not that you've made a bad argument. It's that legal reasoning has limits, and you now understand them a little better than you did before.

Nor should you infer that legal reasoning is a hopeless maze. People often say that the Socratic method teaches you that there are no easy answers. That's not true; there are plenty of easy answers. Here's one: can Congress require citizens to pray to a particular deity? Of course not. The hard part is figuring out exactly what principle explains that easy answer. We can say that Congress can't establish a religion, or talk about the separation of church and state, but it's hard to figure out what those words actually mean. You'll move quickly from the easy answer to hard questions. (Congress made Thanksgiving a holiday. Is that like requiring prayer?)

There are lots of easy answers in law. But to be a good lawyer, you have to learn not to stop with the easy answers. No principle explains everything, and no argument is without inconsistencies. For every rule, there is a situation where an exception should be made. The ability to push legal reasoning to its limits, and to see those limits clearly, is one of the main things the Socratic method teaches.

3. GET CONFIDENT

Speaking in public, for many people, is frightening. Most lawyers don't speak to groups of a hundred people on a regular basis. But all lawyers speak to someone. (If a lawyer argues alone in a forest, and nobody hears her, it is difficult to bill for the hour.) Being able to articulate legal ideas clearly is useful to every lawyer.

Speaking in class for the first time is terrifying, but most people find that it gets easier. It can be an empowering experience, even if you're called on unexpectedly. As one intimidated student said to a researcher after she'd been called on, "you realize, it's not that bad."[3] Confidence comes not from the professor's overt praise—there rarely is any—but from the simple knowledge that you've spoken intelligently and with some measure of self-possession under difficult circumstances.

In the beginning, you're afraid of being wrong. But if you have a good professor, you'll discover that being wrong is a normal part of thinking about law. It's not just that it's OK to make mistakes; it's *necessary*. Law isn't scientific; you can't reach the right answer to a hard legal question by applying some formula. Trial and error is an essential part of legal reasoning. You get to the best answer by testing a series of arguments, seeing which ones hold up best under different kinds of challenges. Arguments that seem promising fall apart eventually. In class, most arguments will fall apart if the professor keeps talking about them long enough. But that doesn't mean you've done a bad job of legal thinking. On the contrary, it means you're doing this right.

4. LEARN TO DRAW ON OTHER PEOPLE'S JUDGMENT

Socratic discussion is not, ideally, a form of combat. Elizabeth Garrett writes that classes shouldn't be "a destructive tournament where gladiators of unequal power and experience vie to the death."[4] The idea behind the Socratic method is *cooperative*—the professor draws not just on her own knowledge and experience, but also on students' own insights, to construct a full picture of the law.

If the method is really cooperative, class will be exciting. Students always offer thoughts the professor doesn't expect. Good professors let the class share their surprise, and incorporate the new ideas into the conversation. This kind of cooperative learning is a great introduction to the kind of thinking lawyers do in the real world.

In a good law practice, you talk to the people you work with about the law you're working on. Your colleagues will often see the law differently than you do. You'll adjust your ideas, or they'll adjust theirs, or both. The way you get to a solid understanding of any legal idea is by testing it against other people's judgment. So you want to learn to have good legal conversations. You want to learn how to absorb other people's legal ideas. Class can help you with that.

5. TRAIN YOUR INSTINCTS

Law school teaches more than doctrine; it teaches you a feeling for what kinds of legal arguments work, and what kinds don't. Law isn't an exact science; it's a culture, and you can't learn your way around without participat-

ing. Any law school exam question could, in theory, trigger an infinite number of possible arguments; your job is to identify the most interesting ones,
the ones that will seem relevant to your professor. To do that, you'll need a
practical knowledge, a feeling for the material.[5]

The conversations that you have in class are opportunities for you to explore the way your professors and your colleagues react to legal ideas. The
difference between a good legal argument and a bad one can be just a matter
of emphasis. The subtle distinctions that make all the difference are hard
to pick up from the printed page. Class is where you develop the gut-level
understanding that makes good lawyers good.

6. GET A BETTER SENSE OF YOUR PROFESSIONAL IDENTITY

Speaking in class can also help you understand what kind of a lawyer you
want to be. If you love the challenge of answering your professor's questions, you might decide you want to be a litigator—a lawyer who represents
clients during lawsuits—because litigators have to stand up and answers
questions from judges that can be much like traditional Socratic questioning in law school. (Argument in appellate courts, in particular, is much like
Socratic questioning, except that appellate judges don't call on members of
the audience at random.)

If you don't like speaking in class, think about why. It may be that you
don't enjoy the performance of it. Or it may be that class requires a lot of
improvising, and you'd rather think things through before you say them.
Class can help you discover what you *don't* want to do. That's valuable too.
But it might just be that you have a bad professor. Be careful: don't let bad
professors change your career path.

7. BUILD RELATIONSHIPS WITH PROFESSORS

Finally, speaking in class is an important way of building relationships with
professors. It's extremely likely that in the course of your job searches—
both for summer jobs during law school and for eventual full-time work
afterward—you'll find it helpful to know a law professor who's been impressed with your well-built arguments, your careful reasoning, your thorough reading skills, your open-mindedness, or some other capacity that
you displayed in class discussion. Class discussion is one of the places where
professors get to see these skills in action.

When Socrates Has Fangs

I've painted a rosy picture of the Socratic method's possibilities so far. You've probably heard horror stories about the law school classroom, and some of them are true. But most professors aren't ghouls. They don't want to hurt you; they want to teach you. They're human beings, doing their best at an extremely difficult job. Try to see them this way.

Remember that you're in a new social environment—one in which taboos you've grown up with are often violated. In most social settings, it's extremely rude to tell someone that their answer to a question is irrelevant and wrong. But that's a routine part of law school class interactions, because it's a routine part of judicial proceedings. Your professor may be trying to teach you to speak concisely and directly, the way lawyers often need to— which may mean beginning with "The last thing you said was wrong, and here's why." The taboos you carry into law school from other social settings may make you feel attacked when in fact you're being trained.

Besides, even a good professor sometimes gets angry, or fails to make sense, or tries a pedagogical experiment that works out badly. When class is alienating or confusing, you'll be best equipped to make sense of it all if you're willing to give the professor another chance.

Still, it's important not to let your confidence suffer if the professor is the one making a hash of things. It's easy to blame yourself for feeling lost or frustrated if you don't understand what's gone wrong. Here are some of the things that can go wrong in law school classes, and what you can do about them.

THE BEFUDDLER

Class discussion will often leave you feeling lost. You're supposed to feel *some* confusion; that's what learning feels like. But in some classes, you'll go past confusion and into despair.

If you're feeling confused, don't be afraid to ask your professor directly for help. I once saw a class burst into applause when a student raised his hand and said, "Professor, I'm sorry, but I really didn't understand what you just said." The professor had been maddeningly obtuse, but everyone had been a little too intimidated to admit they didn't understand. Professors may be grateful to students who help them see where they've lost the class. And, anyway, one of the best things you can learn as a lawyer is how to admit when you're lost.

Sometimes the law will begin to feel so hopelessly muddled and arbitrary that you'll be tempted to conclude that no question has an answer, or at least no answer good enough for your professor. That would be an un-fortunate conclusion. There are difficult questions in law, but a good class will give you tools to approach those difficult questions—not just leave you feeling intimidated by how difficult they are. The best professors know that if they dissect students' answers too aggressively, sending the message that no answer can ever be good enough, students can become timid about tak-ing any position at all.

If you're feeling overwhelmed by uncertainty, or the professor seems to reject every thought that comes from a student's mouth, bear in mind what Phillip Areeda said about how law school classes should be taught: "[W]henever a student seems very uncertain as to how to answer or seems wary, tell him with a smile: I will press you however you answer; take any position to get us started and we will see where it goes."[6] This is supposed to be the spirit of the Socratic method. If your professor forgets this, and rips into someone with gusto, try to remember that even the best arguments can be torn apart. It doesn't mean you're doing a bad job.

THE BASIC MEASURE OF CONTRACT DAMAGES IS . . . ANYONE? ANYONE?

Sometimes class discussion stops being a conversation between professor and students, and becomes more like a game of guess-what-I'm-thinking. When this happens, the professor isn't asking students for their analysis of legal questions; she's just asking students to fill in the blanks at the end of her sentences. "Of course, we saw a similar approach in an earlier case. And that case was . . . anyone? Anyone? . . . No . . . No . . . Yes, that's right, *Marbury v. Madison*."

This approach is usually boring. It can also be confusing and demoral-izing. Say you raise your hand to answer the question about which earlier case had a similar approach. But the case you're thinking of isn't *Marbury*. You might have had some real insight into similarities with a different case. But if the professor is just playing fill-in-the-blank, she'll say "no" and move on without stopping. You're left feeling confused (why wasn't your case the similar one?) and self-critical (why didn't I see the right answer?). But you had a really interesting thought.

The trick is to recognize that when professors play fill-in-the-blank and pass quickly over your ideas, they're not rejecting them. They just had a spe-cific answer in mind, and yours wasn't it. So you shouldn't blame yourself. One professor at Harvard, early in his career, devised a flowchart of every possible answer to every possible question he asked in class, and every pos-sible answer to every possible follow-up, all leading eventually to the point he wanted to make.[7] If the professor doesn't make clear that this is what she's doing—using students' brains like instruments in an orchestra, trying to elicit the right note at the right point in the performance—students who volunteer comments can be left feeling slighted and alienated when the professor seems to reject their ideas.

TERRIFYING DETAILS

Some professors question students relentlessly about the details of the reading. They seem to spend a lot of time in class focusing on the specific facts of the case, and its procedural history. Only after long discussions of details does the class finally turn to the legal propositions students have been struggling to distill. When a professor spends a lot of time focusing on details, it can cause several bad reactions.

Some students respond by getting mad and tuning out: if the professor isn't going to teach the black-letter law, why should they pay attention? But the only way to understand a case is to understand its facts and the arguments it considered. Class discussions often focus on the specific facts of a case, and the specific arguments parties offered, for good reason: it's extremely difficult to understand the proposition a case stands for unless you know exactly what was at stake. Not only are the trivial details important to understanding the propositions—they're also where the real pleasure of reading cases is often to be found. Some of the real-life events you'll read about in your casebooks are so weird that they'd never have worked as fiction.

But it would also be a mistake to let yourself be drawn too deeply into the weeds. You probably don't need to retain all of the details of any case for the exam. When class discussion focuses on the details, remember *why* you're focusing on them: for the light they shed on the proposition the case stands for. Some students are so intimidated by class discussion that they devote most of their study time to details, instead of to the propositions that they'll need on the exams. Don't let the intensity of class discussion fool you into retaining more than you need.

How do you tell when it's important to focus on details, and when it's OK to let them go? The trick is remembering your goal. If you're studying a case because you expect a professor to grill you on it in the morning, think about what you've seen of that professor so far, and study the details you think she might consider fair game. But if you've looked at her old exams, and you have a sense of the level of detail she expects students to produce at the end of the semester, you might well decide that many of the details you study for class can be safely forgotten once the class is over.

Remember that although class can be frightening, it's usually not a significant part of your grade. But remember, too, that if your professor thinks the details of a case are worth focusing on, it's because she thinks you'll benefit in some way from that kind of discussion. Try to figure out why she thinks that. Is she trying to teach you that obscure details can have a major effect on how a case's proposition is later interpreted? Is she trying to get you into the habit of reading carefully? Consider possibilities like these before you decide that she's focusing on trivia because she's malicious.

POISONOUS AIR

Sometimes a bad class experience is more the students' fault than the professor's. Law school classrooms can become too competitive; instead of trying to learn, students talk to show off. At worst, students who speak try to undermine each other, or make snide comments, creating an atmosphere in which other students are afraid to give voice to their ideas. If you find yourself in a class like this, don't be drawn in. You can't change your colleagues, but you can refuse to play along.

THE INQUISITION

I said that most law professors aren't ghouls, but of course a few of them are. It's easy to find awful stories about abusive professors. Two lawyers write, for example, "One professor we know made it a point to reduce at least one student to tears on the first day of class every semester."[8] That professor is a bad human being. And a terrible law professor.

A subtler problem is the professor who exploits students' mistakes by continuing to interrogate a student when it's clear that she can't go any further. As Areeda wrote, "continuing the questioning of one student who is excessively confused or at loose ends is bad teaching, embarrassing the student and the class and ending the dialectical momentum."[9] If a professor continues questioning a student who is obviously bewildered, nobody's learning anything. If this happens to you, try not to blame yourself. Everyone gets flustered and confused sometimes; it's nothing to be ashamed of.

Some professors think they should teach students to toughen up by being as harsh as judges will be.[10] That strikes me as silly. Some judges are downright abusive, or racist, or corrupt. Some are completely insane. Nobody thinks law school professors should train students by imitating *those* extremes. Or do they? One New York City lawyer writes, "A well-conceived law school education serves one purpose only: to prepare you to confront the abuse of being a lawyer and prevail."[11] But abuse doesn't build confidence.

It builds defensiveness, self-doubt, and a compulsive need to cover one's posterior. These are not lawyerly virtues.

Teaching students to think of authority figures as the enemy is profoundly unhelpful. The best litigators are those who turn oral arguments into amicable conversations with judges. The worst are those who think so defensively that they hear every question as an attack—and speak so aggressively that they sound like they're attacking someone even when they're asserting a simple proposition on which everyone agrees. These are common mistakes; it's not at all unusual to see a nervous lawyer misinterpret a judge's softball question as an attack, and deny something that would have helped the lawyer's case. Tough-love professors train students to see authority figures fearfully and resentfully, leading them to just this kind of mistake. Most oral arguments do not involve abuse from the judge. Professors who play bad cop are trying to prepare you for those rare abusive arguments at the expense of preparing you for all the rest.

What law students need isn't immunity from contempt. It's legal skills. What gives students confidence is understanding the law and being good at legal argument, not experience tolerating derision. If you have a professor who is really mean—who is contemptuous of students, or mocks them, or humiliates them—then don't volunteer to speak in class. You should expect to be challenged in law school, but you have every right to be treated with respect.

GIVE YOUR PROFESSORS THE PRESUMPTION OF INNOCENCE

Do not, however, lightly conclude that your professor is being vicious. It's appropriate for the professor to ask difficult questions, and a curt style can sometimes be part of a teaching method that is, in the end, extremely helpful. Even the professors who are harsher than they should be might have something useful to teach you.

It's easy to misunderstand what's happening in class, because in ordinary society it's considered quite rude to say, "I think you're wrong, and here's why." But it's a normal part of legal conversations. When your professor tears your argument apart, even if she does it gently and compassionately, you may feel like it's your heart being sliced. Learning to feel comfortable in debate—learning not to take these things personally—is an important part of legal training. So try to see your professor's sharp questions as helpful practice, not rudeness.

In general, the presumption of innocence is a good approach to classes. Your professor might turn out to be mean or confusing. But you'll get the most out of class if you start off with the assumption that she knows what she's doing, and that she has a lot to offer. Give her the benefit of the doubt.

BEING CRITICAL AND BEING ENGAGED

I want to emphasize this point: it's good to be critical of your professors and of the way law school is taught. Some professors really are quite bad, and there are plenty of legitimate criticisms of law school. So you shouldn't be afraid to question your law school experience and the way they manage it. A student who passively accepts the way things are is likely to feel helpless when things stop making sense. Students who are critical of the process are *engaged.* They're more likely to find ways to get the most out of law school, because they're thinking actively about what works and what doesn't.

Being engaged in this way, though, means avoiding both the extremes of passive acceptance and unthinking contempt. As Karl Llewellyn wrote, "There is indeed no known way to muddy the message of such a document as a judicial opinion more effectively [than] by approaching it with scorn."[12] If you spend your study time mumbling about how stupid the whole process is—if your thoughts are nothing but clouds of resentment and rage—you're wasting time that could be spent thinking about how to approach your studies. The same thing is true of classes: if you sit in the back row fuming about how incomprehensible the professor is, you'll probably miss the moment when she starts making sense.

FEAR ITSELF

Even if you understand intellectually that the professor's questions are well intentioned, and that speaking in class is irrelevant to your grade, many students find classes an alienating, even disturbing experience. If you find class discussion hostile, try to keep it in perspective.

Remember how profoundly unimportant class really is. It's not (in most classes) graded. And what makes you a good lawyer isn't your ability to stand up to Socratic grilling. It's your ability to make sense of legal ideas, *wherever you do that best.* Some people think well under stress; others think best in calmer moments. There's nothing wrong with being a person who thinks best when they're calm.

In fact, the things that alienate you about class discussion may be the things that make you a good lawyer. The shy, careful students who feel excluded from class discussion may become great lawyers because of precisely the qualities that keep them silent in class: they're careful, they take their time, they have little patience for silly rituals of battle. If you think there's too much ego involved in the preening display of knowledge that some law students think professors want to see, good. Lawyers' egos have lost a lot of cases.

In the daily narrative of law school, class discussion takes on a huge significance. It's the arena in which you spend the most time with the person who'll be grading you, and it's your main professional interaction with your peers. You feel like you're being judged on it. But class discussion is usually ungraded. You're free to make mistakes; you're free to experiment with speaking just to see what happens. You're free to use class discussion in whatever way you can.

That is why Zen teachers traditionally create problems where none exist. If they didn't, and everything remained smooth and harmonious, with tranquil and misty landscapes and twittering birds, then nobody would learn anything.

JOHN DAIDO LOORI

9 Listening in Class

The last chapter was about the experience of speaking in class. This one is about listening. Listening is a different skill, and one that's much more relevant to your exams. Learning to become a good listener is crucial in law school, and equally so in lawyering. The Socratic method, if it's working well, can help teach you to listen.

Socratic questioning spurs you to listen actively when your colleagues are being cross-examined. It's not just that you might be called on next; it's that your natural empathy compels you to imagine yourself in the role of the student on the hot seat. When the professor asks someone a question, you scramble to come up with the answer, just as if you were the one on the spot. You get the most out of class that way, because you don't just sit passively, recording information; you listen intently, skeptically, urgently, as if the answers mattered. That's how a good lawyer listens to everything.

At the beginning of the book I said that getting good grades means thinking about everything you do during the semester in terms of how it's relevant to the exam. This is particularly true of class discussion. It's important to understand how class discussion helps you develop the skills you'll need on the exam, and the repertoire of propositions you'll be tested on.

First, class discussion helps you get hold of the propositions you're distilling for the exam. It's not just that you'll hear new propositions in class, although that does happen sometimes. It's that class discussion will help you whittle down cases to their essential propositions, and help you situate those propositions in a broader understanding of the course.

Class discussion will also help you develop your issue spotting and argument skills. These skills are harder to develop on your own. But they're just as crucial.

Classes Are a Source of Propositions

The most important thing to remember about class discussion is what *isn't* important about it. Some classes will give you the idea that you're supposed to learn, and take notes on, every factual and procedural detail of whatever case you're discussing. But that's hardly ever true.

Most professors ask detailed questions during class not because you need to know all those details, but to make sure you've read the case accurately, and to reinforce the message that sometimes a key fact is buried deep within a case. Socratic cross-examination should be a lesson in how to read carefully and well. But do not take it to mean that you need to assimilate and retain *all* of the facts and arguments in any particular case.

Your fellow students may also make this harder. Some of them, when called on by the professor, will give answers that sound like they've spent the last four years studying the prior night's reading. This will make you feel worried—you're being graded against these people. Worse, it will make you want to study the details that your classmates seem so well prepared to regurgitate on a moment's notice. Don't. They're wasting their time. The point is to be prepared for the exam, not to sound like a know-it-all in class.

Instead of making you feel pressured to learn trivial details, class discussion should help you see how to ignore them. Classes help you see which propositions matter to your professor, the person who writes your exam—and, by implication, which propositions don't matter. If your professor talks about a proposition in class, she probably thinks it's important enough to put on the exam. If it comes up in two classes in a row, it's a safe bet that you'll need it on the exam.[1] If it never comes up in class, and it's not relevant to what you talked about in class, it's probably not worth spending much time on.

The bad news is that class discussion is itself something you'll have to learn to distill. Sometimes your professor will use class to explain important propositions, especially general ones about theory or philosophy. Other times, she'll say, "By the way, this case represents an unusual approach; the majority of states come out the other way." You may get points on the exam for knowing that. Some students I knew seemed to think there was a rule that professors could only test you on propositions that appeared in the casebook. They were outraged when professors would say, "This isn't in the reading, but you should also know that . . ." There's no rule against this. Professors are indeed allowed to tell you new propositions in class.

In general, though, from the perspective of the exam, classes are an enormous help in distilling the propositions you'll be tested on. When the professor begins a sentence with "The rule is . . .," she is giving you the proposition she expects you to have ready when you take the exam. Her formulation will often be more clear than what you were able to squeeze from the reading. But even if it's not more clear, it's more *relevant*. Just as each student will compose a different version of the propositions, each professor will compose them somewhat differently. Class discussion is your opportunity to hear how your professor composes the propositions you're studying. It's important to make your version of the propositions compatible with your professor's version, because your professor is the one who'll be judging whether your version of the propositions should get points on the exam.

It can also be useful to hear how other students compose the propositions. It feels frustrating, sometimes, to listen to the professor asking student after student to identify the proposition of a particular case. You sit thinking, I don't care what *they* think—I want to know what *you* think. And, yes, that would be nice. But if the professor nods, or grunts contentedly, you'll know they got it right. And even if the professor doesn't respond at all, it's worth listening to the way your colleagues formulate the propositions. They'll compose the ideas in ways you hadn't thought of, and you'll benefit from hearing alternate approaches.

Class can help you distill the cases even if the professor doesn't explicitly state her version of the rule—because you can do it yourself. Try just raising your hand and asking, "I think the rule is such-and-such. Is that right?" If the professor makes a gagging sound, you'll know you need more work. If professors respond coldly to students who dare to ask direct questions in class, try talking to them after class, or during office hours.

Questioning your professor typically goes well if you have specific questions ready. As Llewellyn wrote, "If you come not to milk him like a cow, but for help in a problem you have struggled with, and hard, then what you bring is worth the time you cost."[2] Don't ask your professor, "What's contributory negligence?" Ask, instead, "Assumption of the risk and contributory negligence seem like the same thing to me; what's the difference between the two doctrines?" If you know what your question is, your professor can help bring you to the next level of understanding. Ideally, she'll also help you reflect on your own development, so that you can see how to face the next problem more skillfully. You may find that professors who are implacably Socratic in class are willing to give you straight answers afterward. Even if they're not, it's a great chance to have further conversations in which you can explore the mind of the person who'll be grading you.

And this is how mentoring relationships often develop between students and professors: the student brings the professor a question with which she's obviously been struggling, and the professor is impressed with the struggle. From there a conversation begins.

If you're shy—which, contrary to what you might hear from macho trench lawyers, is a fine thing to be—just go hang around on the fringes of the little group that forms around the professor after class. If the professor asks you whether you have a question, it's perfectly appropriate to say, "Just listening." Depending on the professor, those little sessions can sometimes be more use than the rest of class. The professor may be more open and clear, and it's easier for students and for the professor to talk without the pressure of a hundred colleagues listening.

Class can also help with putting the propositions into context. It can help you fit the propositions together into a coherent whole, so that you really understand the broad topics you've studied. In traditional law school classes, professors try to help you see the big picture not by explaining it to you, but by forcing you to construct it yourself. Professors' questions are often designed to force you to fit two of the doctrines you've learned together. ("How does that relate to what we learned about promissory estoppel, Ms. Anderson?") If you can see how the doctrines relate and overlap, you're seeing the big picture. And fitting the doctrines together is what you'll have to do on the exam, so pay attention.

One way to see the big picture is to notice the currents and themes that your professor sees running through the semester. Many of the best law school professors have a theme for the class. My federal courts class, for example, was an exploration of all of the ways our legal system has made it difficult for litigants to get their cases heard in federal courts. We kept coming back to that theme. It made the class interesting, and gave us a reason to care about each case we read. It also made it much easier to fit the cases together into a bigger theme. Conflict makes a good theme, so good teachers will often use the class to tell a story of a battle between two forces or ideas: two schools of legal thought, or two groups (like landlords and tenants) who often find themselves on opposite sides of the law.

Try to notice the theme your professor develops, and try to incorporate it into your work toward the exam. If the class is fundamentally about a particular idea or recurring theme, and you recognize it, you can distill your notes more effectively because you'll be better at picking the propositions that matter and fitting them into the big picture. And you'll be able to make your exam answers interesting to the professor, because they'll show her that you understood the fundamental conflict that she was trying to illustrate.

Argument and Issue Spotting in Class

You don't go to class just to get the propositions clear. Class also teaches you to argue, not just by forcing students to practice argument themselves (although that helps) but by giving you a chance to hear and evaluate legal arguments by your professor and classmates.

Again, law is a culture, and to understand it you have to be immersed. Llewellyn said, "Pickle yourselves in law—it is your only hope."[3] As you listen to each argument offered in class, and notice the way your professor and your colleagues react to them, you'll develop a better gut sense of what kinds of arguments are persuasive.

The logical side of legal argument is often overvalued by lawyers. We like to think we're a logical profession. So in legal briefs, you'll often see a lawyer saying, "The plaintiff's argument is wrong, as my first brief *demonstrated*"—as if the lawyer had been able to prove formally or empirically that her adversary was wrong. The truth is that formal logic plays a pretty small role in legal argument. Horse sense plays a big one. In class, you see horse sense in action. You begin to develop your professional sense of which arguments work, and why.

Class discussion also helps you see which arguments are worth making on your exam, by helping you see what kinds of arguments your professor is interested in. Some professors love to talk about inconsistencies in the reasoning behind the doctrines. Others don't care whether cases are coherently reasoned; they just care what the rule is, and if you start deconstructing *Marbury v. Madison* on the exam, they'll think you're an arrogant little snoot and mark you down for it. Learn what's important to them, because it will affect what you choose to discuss on exams.

Finally, and somewhat more subtly, class discussions also teach issue spotting. One of the more plausible justifications for the Socratic technique of endless questioning is that it teaches you how to ask those kinds of questions yourself. Learning to spot issues is one of your biggest challenges: it's crucial on the exam, and important for lawyers in practice. The endless questions you hear in class are models for your own thinking.

Students often get furious at professors who ask questions and never give answers. And endless questioning can make for an extremely boring class. But questions are useful pieces of information themselves, apart from their answers. Every question your professor asks is an example of issue spotting. Learn to listen and try to anticipate. After a while, it should seem obvious to you what kinds of questions your professor is going to ask next. That's how you'll know you're getting good at issue spotting.

You can study the rules until your eyes fall out of your head, but if you cannot recall which rule fits your particular situation just before some large ship hits you broadside, then a study of the rules has failed you at the worst possible time.

CAPT. JOHN W. TRIMMER, *How to Avoid Huge Ships*

10 Notes and Outlines

Law school exams test you on your notes.

To do well on exams, you'll need to have easy access to the propositions you've painstakingly distilled from the reading and class discussions. Your notes are where you keep those propositions. During the exam, you'll rely on your notes, because the primary sources are too incomprehensible, too scattered, and too inaccessible. Your notes, not your casebook, are what you will study when you prepare for the exam.

So you'll need to develop the habit of collecting in your notes all the propositions you think might help on exams. In class, you'll take down the important things your professor says. When you chat with a professor and pick up a bit of insight, you'll head off to your computer and note it down. When you do your nightly reading, your notes will be by your side. When you're skimming through a study guide on the subway, and something suddenly clicks, you'll try to note it down before you've forgotten it.

But your notes aren't just a dumping ground for information. They are a project in their own right. They're where you compose the law. They are themselves a thing to be composed. Your notes aren't just recordings of what happened in class, or summaries of cases; they're your version of the law you study.

This chapter suggests a method for distilling and outlining your notes. I said earlier that I wanted to show you what choices you'd have to make, rather than giving you answers; in this chapter, I bend that rule, because the best way to explain how notes and outlines work is to show you one successful system. I hope you'll treat this as a starting point for your own reflections on approaches for studying, rather than as a roadmap to be rigidly followed. On the other hand, I also hope the method doesn't sound too labor intensive to be attractive; I hope to persuade you by the end that it's an efficient method, largely by showing you how it allows you to dispense with the traditional work of outlining your courses at the end of the semester.

Here's a summary of what follows—a study method condensed into four sentences:

- Before class, take sketchy notes, writing down only what's necessary to follow class discussion.
- After class, edit your notes—give each proposition its own entry, and a title that expresses the proposition clearly.
- Then insert headings and subheadings that help you see the bigger structure of the law you're studying.
- Finally, use the table-of-contents function in your word processor to generate an outline automatically.

The main feature of this system is the process of going back over your notes after class discussion, and working them into a form that will be useful to you later in the semester. Different systems, no doubt, will work for different students. But it's hard to imagine any successful system that doesn't include some process of distilling and organizing notes.

Distilling and Organizing Your Notes

To give you a sense of how notes might usefully be organized, let's start this chapter with an example of some well-organized notes from a course on criminal law. These notes deal with the *actus reus*—guilty act—element of crimes. Crimes generally must involve the commission of some act by the criminal, although, as you might expect, complicated questions arise about this. These notes deal with one such question: whether the guilty acts must be voluntary—and what, exactly, "voluntary" means.

As you look at these notes, pay particularly close attention to the headings and subheadings, and to the titles that appear over the entries. (The entries are the stuff you actually typed into your computer while you were reading the cases and sitting in class; they appear in brackets here.)

Notes on the Guilty Act Requirement

    A. The Guilty Act Must Be Voluntary
       1. The Voluntariness Requirement

A voluntary act is required: Model Penal Code § 2.01

[Here are the notes you jotted down when you read the Model Penal Code—probably just the text of the provision itself—as well as the notes you took during class discussion of the code provision.]

    2.   Blackouts and Automatism Are Complete Defenses
        Unconsciousness while in shock is a complete defense to murder:
        People v. Newton

[Here are the notes you jotted down while you were reading *People v. Newton,* and during the class discussion that covered it.]

        Automatism (veteran's blackouts) is a complete defense to murder:
        State v. Jerrett

[Here are the notes you jotted down while you were reading *State v. Jerrett,* and during the class discussion that covered it.]

    3.   Sudden Heat Is Not a Complete Defense
        "Sudden heat" (insane rage) only reduces murder to manslaughter:
        Baird v. State[1]

[Here are the notes you jotted down while you were reading *Baird v. State,* and during the class discussion that covered it.]

First, notice the headings and subheadings: Every heading in this outline is a *legal proposition,* not just a concept. Legal propositions are the units of your thought. If subheading 3 just said, "Sudden Heat," it wouldn't help you remember what the rule on sudden heat is. Formulating these headings and subheadings is an important part of your work on your notes, because it's important that your headings and subheadings have enough information in them to be useful. This will often mean that your headings and subheadings—like your entry titles—aren't just phrases or concepts like "Guilty Acts" or "Voluntariness." They'll be propositions, like "The Guilty Act Must Be Voluntary." This will be much more useful when you're studying for the exam (which is to say, throughout the semester). When you write the heading out as a proposition, you're forced to state the rule in your own words. Also, when you come back to this part of your notes, or even skim past it, you'll see the rule you need and internalize it a little more deeply.

As for the overall structure of your notes: As you begin your semester, your notes will naturally follow the organization of the syllabus. You may find, though, that it makes sense to break free from the syllabus and order your notes in some other way. In some classes, for example, you'll have a short introductory unit that gives you an overview of some key concepts, and then you'll return to those concepts throughout the semester. It doesn't make sense to keep those concepts scattered in your notes. Merge the early discussion and the later discussion.

Spend some time playing with the overall organization of your notes. Seeing the big picture of the course is an important part of being ready for exams. You can learn a lot by asking yourself what structure for your notes makes the most sense, and looking for creative ways to reorganize them. The more you fiddle the better.

The most important fiddling you'll do, though, is not with headings and subheadings; it's with the titles of the individual entries in your notes. So let's move on, now, to those entries. Looking at the sample notes above, you can see that they're each given in the form of a proposition, just as the headings and subheadings were. The principle on which the sample notes above are organized is this: *one entry per proposition.*

First, let's talk about why it's important to organize your notes into separate entries. Some students don't have separate entries in their notes—just a date for each day's class, followed by an undifferentiated mass of sentences. Other students create a different file on their computer for each day of class notes. But it's extremely difficult to study notes like these, and impossible to draw anything useful from them during an exam. The purpose of note taking is to put all of the law together so you can distill it into one useful whole. You need to see the big picture. If your notes are all in one file, you can even use your word-processing program to automatically generate a table of contents—an outline—for you. (We'll talk about that soon.) Use one file. If that file gets too big for your word-processing program, use two.

Next, let's talk about why the title of each entry is a proposition. The unit of legal thinking is the proposition, so it makes sense for the unit of legal note taking to be the proposition too. That's why the sample notes above gave a title to each entry; every proposition (and, in the sample, every case) got a title in which the proposition was distilled. These titles are the most important part of the process of note taking.

Remember, the purpose of notes is to help you have the legal propositions at hand when you take the exam. You don't want to spend time distilling propositions in your head during the exam; you want them already distilled into neat, concise propositions, ready to be dropped right into your exam answer. The titles of your notes are a good place to do this predistilling. Instead of titling the entry *"Roe v. Wade,"* title it something like:

Implicit right to privacy includes right to abortion: *Roe v. Wade.*

The proposition you want is right there in the title. I've put the name of the case at the end, because the case name is worth putting in titles too. You may want to cite it on the exam, and it'll be much easier to follow class discussion if the titles of each entry say what case you're talking about. But it's much less important than the actual proposition. (The exam is not going to ask you who sued Wade.)

Titling the entries in your notes forces you to think about the proposition each case stands for. If you title an entry in your notes *"Roe v. Wade,"* you don't have to do any real thinking about the proposition the case stands for. Propositional titles help you learn by forcing you to restate the law in your own words. (When you try to create a concise statement of the law you just read, you'll often realize you didn't understand the case well enough to summarize it in a sentence.) And if the entries in your notes have well-distilled titles, you'll learn the law a little better every time you look them over.

Distilling forces you to decide what's important about the case. While some cases are offered mainly to teach you a rule, others are offered to show you fact patterns that illustrate how a rule is enforced. So when you review your notes, ask yourself, why did I read this case? If the point was to learn a rule, give the entry in your notes a title like this:

> Groom left at the altar can't sue bride for failing to marry him: *Prey v. Kruse.*[2]

(He can, however, sue for the cost of the cake.)

If the point of the case was to offer a fact pattern that illustrates a legal doctrine, try to give it a title that summarizes the illustrative facts:

> Hotel guest attacked by mongoose: not foreseeable: *Woods-Leber v. Hyatt.*[3]

The facts of *Woods-Leber* illustrate the doctrine of foreseeability, under which you can only sue people for negligence if the injury they failed to prevent was reasonably foreseeable. The plaintiff, a hotel guest, was attacked by a mongoose. The court said that hotel management could not reasonably have been expected to foresee the attack. Once you've read the case, you don't need to say all that; the simple distilled summary above should be enough. Of course, you might be wrong about what's important in a given case, but so what? If you're wrong, at least now your mistake is identified in bold type where you can more easily find and recognize it later.

Do the same thing for propositions that don't come from cases. If you read or discuss a scholarly article that contains a significant proposition, give it its own entry in your notes, and summarize its basic proposition in the title of the entry:

> Jury nullification can be an appropriate response to racially disparate law enforcement: Paul Butler.[4]

The title of the article probably doesn't matter, because on the exam, you'll just want to say, "Professor Butler argues such-and such." So just list the author and his or her proposition.

The same thing applies to statutes, which often contain many more propositions of law per paragraph than any case does. A statute might, for example, have a rule and an exception built into it. When you learn a proposition and an exception, give them each their own entry:

> No false statements or cover-ups in any matter within the jurisdiction of the US govt: 18 USC 1001(a)

> Exception for statements of parties in judicial proceedings: 1001(b)

The advice I gave earlier, about the importance of restating propositions in your own words, still applies: you want to be able to say in your own words what a statute requires. But be careful: the precise language of statutes often matters a great deal. If you're answering a question on a statute during the exam, be sure to look at the real language, not just your summary.

Professorial digressions may also deserve an entry in your notes. When discussing the crime of homicide, for example, your professor might say, "But before we get into that, what does it mean to say something is an element of a crime?" You then spend half an hour discussing whether the elements of a crime must be set forth in a statute. Your professor thinks it's important for you to understand that courts sometimes add elements to crimes, beyond what's set forth in the statute. If your professor spends half an hour on it, it's a proposition worth preserving. Give it a separate title in your notes:

> Courts can add elements to statutory crimes: Prof's digression.

Later when you come back to distill your notes, move it to a place in your notes where it fits intelligibly, like a beginning section on "General Principles." On the exam, you'll look for ways to work those propositions in.

The principle of one entry per proposition means that cases with more than one proposition get more than one entry in your notes. For example, a teacher might care both what a given case said and what the general philosophy underlying the case was. In that case, make two entries in your notes, one for each proposition. For example, your professor might think you should know several things about *Brown v. Board of Education,* and so your notes might contain at least two entries:

Meaning of 14th Amendment can change over time: *Brown v. Board*

Segregation in public schools violates right to equal protection: *Brown v. Board*

That might look awkward at first. But if you're going to use a case for more than one proposition on the exam, it deserves more than one entry in your notes.

This sounds like a time-consuming approach, I know. And it does take some time. But it takes less time than case briefing; in fact, the process of titling the entries in your notes is a *replacement for case briefing*. At the beginning of your first semester, you'll want to do full case briefs for a little while, just to get familiar with the separate elements of cases. But you'll quickly want to stop briefing, because you don't need to retain all of the elements of each case. Once you've gotten the hang of titling the entries in your notes, there's no reason to brief cases anymore. In fact, as the next section explains, once you've gotten the hang of titling the entries in your notes, you won't need to make course outlines either. That's the real reason it saves time.

Outlines

Law students traditionally make sense of their course material by creating an outline of each course. Outlines contain a semester's worth of law, boiled down to simple propositions. They're often organized in bullet-point format. Outlining has advantages and disadvantages. On one hand, it's extremely important to review your course material as the semester goes on, and you cannot do well on exams unless you distill your notes down into a usable form. On the other hand, there may be more efficient ways to create a distilled version of your notes.

This chapter will suggest a way of integrating the outlining process with the process of note taking. If you're willing to spend a little extra time editing your notes after each class, as the last section suggested, you should be able to save a lot of time at the end of the semester—and understand the law much better by the time you get there.

The last section said that your notes must be distilled to be useful. I suggested that you give each entry in your notes a well-distilled title, and organize them under headings and subheadings. If you do that, you won't need to create a separate outline at all. Your outline will emerge organically from your notes.

First, let's focus on how outlines are supposed to help you on the exam. The purpose of an outline is to sit by your side as you take your exam—or, if the exam is closed-book exam, to sit by your side right up until you take it. The outline is supposed to be your main resource during the exam. It will give you the legal propositions you need, in conveniently distilled form. But it will also be the key to issue spotting, because the headings in your outline will amount to a list of the major areas covered in the course.

In a contracts outline, for example, there should be a few big headings corresponding to the major subject areas you've studied: "Elements of Contract," "Damages," and a few more. Under each heading, you'll have subheadings, like "A Valid Contract Requires an Offer," "A Valid Contract Requires an Acceptance," and so on. These headings will make issue spotting easy. On the exams, you'll use them as a checklist for your issue spotting. As you work on each question, you'll look at these headings—this list of major issues covered in the course—and if there are major issues that you haven't yet mentioned in your answer, look again.

If you have notes that are distilled and organized in the way the last section suggested, there is no need to create an outline. Most word-processing programs will do it for you. To see how, you'll have to spend about ten minutes learning how to create one automatically. Many word-processing programs call it a *table of contents*. Just go to the "help" function, and search for instructions on how to create a table of contents or an outline. What used to take law students weeks now takes less than five seconds.

If this computer trick won't work for you, that's OK. Instead of generating your own table of contents automatically with your word-processing program, you can go through your notes and copy each title and heading into an outline. It'll take a lot longer, but that might be a good thing. You'll certainly pay more attention to each proposition of law if you're copying them all one by one into an outline. It might be a useful exercise.

And there are lots of ways to organize your notes. You might accomplish the same goals more easily with other kinds of computer programs, or other outlining strategies altogether. The point is to make sure you're distilling your notes into a form that makes the relevant legal propositions easily available to you at exam time. The system I've described worked well for me, but you might be able to do better. Read other books, talk to friends, experiment with different approaches.

Now that we've seen how outlines can be automatically generated—and how they depend on and complement your own work distilling the propositions—we can say something about other people's outlines. Toward the end of the semester, you'll probably notice students swapping outlines. In some study groups, each member will be assigned to outline one class, so that the whole group has outlines for every class, but no one has to do more than one outline. (That's how they do it in *The Paper Chase*.) Looking at other students' outlines can be useful, but it's a bad idea to let someone else do your outlining for you.

Other students' outlines are good for the same thing other students are good for: showing you someone else's view of the law. Sometimes you can understand the law better by looking at it from another person's perspective. Sometimes your colleagues will be wrong about the law, but that's OK; their misunderstandings can help show you your own. Other students will also be right about the law in places where you're wrong, and that will obviously help too. And other students will pick up things you didn't. So looking at other students' outlines can give you useful perspective on your own understanding of the law. But it won't substitute for your own process of distilling the law, any more than someone else can go to the gym on your behalf. The process of collecting the law in your notes, titling each entry in a way that concisely states the proposition, and organizing it all with a table of contents is how you learn.

Whether or not you adopt the method I'm suggesting, it's a bad idea to wait until the end of the semester to start outlining. First, waiting won't work. If you didn't understand things the first time, you won't be able to speed through them in one great burst in the final week. Second, if you're distilling at the end of the semester, then you've been reading each assignment without the benefit of having distilled the earlier assignments. You understand things better if you understand what came before. Also, if you're forced to spend the last few weeks of the semester distilling your way through the course, you're missing the opportunity to study in more useful ways. Law school exams will require you to *apply* the law you've learned. So exam preparation should involve applying the law, not just struggling to understand it.

Whatever your approach, outlining should be done piece by piece over the semester, as a natural part of each class assignment.

Jotting Things Down

So far, this chapter has talked about how to organize your notes through the use of headings and subheadings, and how to give effective titles to the entries in your notes. What it hasn't talked about is what goes under those headings, subheadings, and titles: the notes themselves. There are two important questions here: what kind of notes should you take on the reading before you show up in class, and what kind of notes should you take during class?

Some students show up in class with notes that are almost as long as the reading assignment. Detailed notes make sense if your professor is prone

to interrogating students on the details of the reading. But if you're not ex-
pecting a Socratic grilling on the details of the reading, it makes more sense
to take notes that are only as detailed as necessary to help you follow the
discussion.

Your notes can't be distilled until you've had the benefit of class discussion, because class discussion is itself an important part of the information
you're distilling. As an earlier chapter explained, class discussion helps you
identify the relevant propositions and put them in context; this makes distilling after class much easier than distilling before class. The only reason
to take *any* notes before class is to help you understand class discussion, or,
if your professor is prone to grilling you, to withstand the grilling. So take
sketchy notes. Write down only as much as you think you'll need to follow,
and survive, class discussion.

Here's a suggestion to help you take fewer and better notes before class.
Many people take notes as they read, stopping every time they hit a sentence that seems important to summarize it in their notes. But it's hard to
say what matters in a case until you've finished reading it. (As Vladimir
Nabokov said, "Curiously enough, one cannot read a book: one can only
reread it."[5]) Each case probably contains only one or two propositions that
matter. It's easier to pick them out when you've read the whole thing. So it
can be better to take no notes at all until you've read the whole case.

Note taking *during* class presents a more difficult question than note taking before class. Taking notes during class is hard. You're trying to simulta-
neously follow the conversation, summarize it in your head, write it down,
and (sometimes) tamp down the panic at the possibility of being called on.
You'll have to take the best notes you can, distilling on the fly as much as
you can.

Most law students use laptops, which are both a great tool and a terrible
crutch. They're a great tool because they make it easy to revise and distill
on the fly. But they're a terrible crutch because it can be easy to slip into
transcribing class rather than trying to distill it.

A few professors have decided to ban laptops in their classes. It's not just
that they're worried about students surfing the web during class. That's
certainly an issue. But many professors also believe students actually learn
better without laptops. Taking notes on a laptop "encourages verbatim
transcription," explains David Cole, who banned them. The student "tends
to go into stenographic mode and no longer processes information in a way
that is conducive to the give and take of classroom discussion." Cole wants
his students to take notes by hand, because the very clunkiness of handwrit-
ten note taking forces one "to listen, think and prioritize the most important themes."[6] In other words, the laptop ban forces students to distill.

It's true that laptops tend to turn students into stenographers. Most students can type fast enough to transcribe at least significant parts of the class, and if you're transcribing, you're not distilling. The point of class is to help you boil the law down, not to give you another twenty pages of gibberish to sort through. Worst of all, if you just turn off your brain and type, you'll miss the intellectual exchange that really is the point of class. Interestingly, reports from professors who have tried banning laptops tend to indicate that students approved of the ban.[7] I'm sure that class discussions are more lively and engaging when students aren't sitting there, brains turned off, transcribing everything that's said. (Or playing video games.)

That said, I have to admit that the crutch of transcription-style note taking got me through some difficult parts of my first year. In an ideal world, it's better to take concise notes than to transcribe. But what if you have no idea what the professor is talking about? Even the very best students sometimes find class discussion baffling. The style in which law school classes are taught makes it easy to get completely lost. And when you get lost, sometimes the smartest thing to do is start typing.

If you've transcribed an incomprehensible discussion, you'll at least be able to come back to your notes later and try to figure out what it meant. This can be surprisingly easy—legal language sometimes just needs to be repeated once or twice for its meaning to leap forth. (Tape-recording the lectures, if your professor allows it, might be a better alternative.)

There's a tension here, as there often is, between habits that will help you do well in law school and habits that will help you do well as a lawyer. If you wanted to prepare yourself for legal practice, you'd swear off the laptop, because that would compel you to develop your listening skills, instead of your stenography. But if you want to prepare yourself for competitively graded law school exams, transcription can sometimes help. You'll have to pore through lots more notes later, and you won't develop the skill of distilling on the fly that lets you keep the notes shorter in your next class. But if that's the price of understanding what the professor is talking about, it may be worth it.

No matter how good you are at distilling during class, you'll need to return to your notes when it's over. You cannot usefully distill your notes until class discussion is over because class discussion gives you so much information about which propositions matter and how the professor understands them.

This means that the best time to distill and organize your notes is right after class, when the information is fresh in your mind. Whenever you do it, the habit of distilling your notes after class is the single thing most likely to improve your grades and your understanding of the law you've studied. Every night, for me, it was the difference between understanding and not.

It has been found by experience that learning the slide rule can be made most interesting by two or more students' working together and making slide rule practice a game.

CALVIN C. BISHOP, *Slide Rule and How To Use It*

Insanity in individuals is something rare—but in groups, parties, nations and epochs, it is the rule.

FRIEDRICH NIETZSCHE, *Beyond Good and Evil*

11 Ten Ways to Use a Study Group

Nobody is quite sure what study groups are for. On Friday afternoons in a law school cafeteria, one finds a table where bleary-eyed nerds copy each other's marginalia and compare insights in hushed voices. At the next table, jocks talk about tequila and bounce tennis balls off each other's foreheads. Both of these things are called "study groups."

And rightly so. Study groups are an ungraded activity. What happens in your study group stays in your study group. You're completely free to do whatever helps you in whatever sense you most need to be helped. So the question is, what do you need the study group for? If you're going to be in a study group, figure out why, and talk about it with the others. Study groups can help immensely, but they can also waste time that nobody in law school has to spare.

Choosing what to do with your study group can be a useful process, because it focuses your attention on the question of where you need the most help. Self-awareness is an important quality in a law student, because you have limited resources of time and mental energy and it can be hard to decide where to invest them.

Study groups often don't last through the end of the first semester of law school, because people tend to have different needs and goals. There's nothing wrong with that. But it's a good idea to talk about what you want to get out of your group, early and often. That way, nobody gets offended when priorities differ.

Rather than tell you what to do with a study group, this chapter will give you a list of possibilities. Add to them your own ideas. Whatever works best is what you should do.

A skeptic I know suggested that I begin this chapter by saying, "Out of collective ignorance, wisdom does not flow." But it turns out that it sometimes does. In one study that asked students to solve a logical-reasoning problem, only 9 percent of students were able to solve the problem on their own, but when they broke into groups of five or six people to discuss it, 70 percent of the groups solved the problem. About two-thirds of the students got the problem wrong on their own but changed their answer to the correct answer after group discussion. Out of ten groups, three of them got the answer right even though *no student in the group had been able to figure it out on their own.*[1] So wisdom can sometimes flow out of collective ignorance. Here are ten ways to get the most out of your group—just to get you started:

1. Figure Out What Propositions You've Learned

Probably the simplest use for a study group is to look over your notes from the week, and ask each other what you thought you learned. You'll encounter a dozen legal propositions or more in any given week. When you go around the circle and try to sum up what those propositions were, it can be amazing how infrequently you all agree.

The cases you read are often garbled and difficult, and the class discussion is sometimes less than illuminating. It may sound like a waste of time to sit around asking each other, "What did you think that case said?" If it *is* a waste of time, you shouldn't do it. But sometimes trying to repeat back what you learned is the only way to find out that you didn't actually understand it.

2. Ask What Propositions Were Important

A slight variation on the first idea is to focus your discussion on which propositions are relevant and important. Go through the cases, and ask why you spent so much time in class on a particular issue. What matters?

3. See the Big Picture

Another slight variation on the first idea: Talk about how the propositions you've learned fit into the big picture of the class. "So, let's review what we've learned so far. First, we covered intentional torts—which was *Goat v. Cow, Compare v. Contrast,* and *Decency v. Yoo*—and then we started on negligence, which was *Peter v. Tom, Style v. Substance,* and *Stinky v. Clean.*" You'll get disagreement pretty quickly: someone will think *Stinky v. Clean* was a case about damages, not about negligence, and by the end of the discussion you'll understand a little better how it all fits together.

4. Practice Issue Spotting

Try to come up with fact patterns in which the issues you've studied are hidden away. One person can be assigned to come up with a fact pattern, and the rest of the group can try to spot the issues in it. Try to invent new situations and new hypotheticals, and see how the rules you've learned might apply to them.

5. Practice Argument

There's always plenty to argue about. Take any case you read, and assign one or two people to argue in favor of its outcome, and one or two people to argue against its outcome. Or make up your own cases.

Or instead of arguing the pros and cons of a case, argue the pros and cons of a legal doctrine. For example, try to argue that the basic concept of a written constitution is a bad idea. (Not all countries have one.) If you can argue against a concept like the Constitution, or the doctrine of negligence, you can feel confident that you understand the reasons behind it. This will come in handy on the exam.

Or argue about anything else on your mind. Study groups are organized opportunities to disagree. Disagreement is how you learn. So argue about what the propositions were, or which ones were important, or how they fit together. Just argue.

6. Practice Exam Taking

At some point in the semester, you'll want to start taking practice exams. Study groups can be an excellent way to get into the habit of exam taking. Also, professors rarely offer or discuss practice exams in class, which means that you never benefit from observing your comrades' exam taking skills in action. (You really do learn a lot about distilling, issue spotting, and argument from watching your classmates attempt them in class.) Different people take exams differently, and you can get a lot out of talking to your classmates about how they approach it.

A study group can be a good motivator. With all the other work to do, it's hard to make yourself sit down to a long, tedious fact pattern. Also, some professors don't put old exams on file. It's impossible to write an exam for yourself and be surprised by it. So you may need your classmates to write practice questions for you.

7. War-Game the Exam

Try to guess what questions your professor will put on the exam. Writing practice questions can be an excellent way to understand what the professor is thinking. War-gaming the exam is a great way to prepare for it. The more heads you have working on this the better. Writing your own exam will lead you into a debate about how your professor is thinking about the exam, and seeing the course from the professor's point of view is what you should be aiming for.

8. Process the Whole Experience

It's unfortunate that many law professors rarely stop to talk about the teaching method they're using. It's a strange method. It bears talking about. The transition you're undergoing in the first few months will require a lot of processing, both cognitive and emotional.

Some parts of the experience are especially central. There's the Socratic method: in the first few weeks of law school, it can be very useful to talk to colleagues about how classes are being taught and what effect that has on you. Classes can be a frightening, mystifying experience. But, as I hope I convinced you earlier, there's a lot to be gained from them. It can help to talk to classmates about how your professors work. What is your professor trying to teach you? Why does she teach the way she does? Was a particular class session helpful or not?

And then there's the broader question of what law school is doing to you as a person. You're becoming a lawyer. What's that like? What does it mean? Are you in control? All of these questions bear talking about. The human experience of law school is real, and complex, and conversation with your colleagues can be one of the best ways to make sense of it.

9. Do Absolutely Nothing Useful

Another perfectly legitimate use for a study group is to do nothing useful at all. Talk about TV, or knit. Blow off steam. Many books will warn you about the dangers of study groups that waste time because people chat instead of working. But wasting three hours isn't necessarily a bad thing.

You need to blow off steam. You need to feel like you're not alone. You need to talk to people about the whole law school experience—not just the work but the *life*—to help your mind and your heart wrap themselves around what you're going through.

Use study groups for whatever you find most useful, and don't be ashamed to acknowledge that you need more help with the stress than with the law. The stress is real, and the value of talking to friends is measureless. This is the opposite of what some people recommend: "It's sink or swim in your first year," warns a typical book about law school, "and you don't want to be somebody's life-ring."[2] I think you *do* want to be somebody's life ring. The friendships that sometimes form in the pressure of the first year are among the greatest rewards law school has to offer. There is nothing wrong with being somebody's life ring, academically or emotionally. Especially if you know that next week they might be yours.

10. Avoid Study Groups Altogether

Finally, you may not want to have a study group. That's fine too. Study groups can be great opportunities, when you're lucky enough to end up in one that shares your goals. But with the wrong people—people whose needs and skills don't fit well with yours—they can frustrating and useless. Study groups are a tool, to be used however you see fit. The ideas listed here are just some of the possible ways to use a study group, and if these or some other idea make sense to you, great. But if you're a rugged individualist, or just someone who'd rather be with a spouse than with your law school classmate, don't feel panicked or ashamed. Do what works for you, and when it stops working, stop doing it.

12 Beyond Traditional Classes

What else do law students do, besides going to traditional classes like the ones offered in the first year? There are two categories to discuss here: nontraditional classes and extracurricular activities. This chapter will give a brief overview of each category, so you can understand what your choices are. The best way to choose is to think about what you're hoping to get out of the experience—in particular, which skills you're hoping to cultivate. Some classes and activities help develop the three traditional legal-reasoning skills on which this book has, so far, focused. Many classes and activities also help develop skills and capabilities beyond traditional legal-reasoning skills—especially practical skills that are important in law practice, but not tested on traditional exams. And some of the classes and activities might help you find a job.

Nontraditional Classes

Law schools have been criticized for more than a hundred years by critics who say that traditional classes don't do enough to prepare students for practice.[1] Traditional classes focus on teaching legal doctrine, but of course lawyers do much more than just argue about legal doctrine; they need to be good at research, writing, negotiating, public speaking, and many other things as well. A particularly influential report by the Carnegie Foundation, released in 2007, argued that law schools have a responsibility to teach students not just the skills of legal reasoning, but also to help them learn practical skills and develop their professional identities.[2] The Carnegie report spurred a great deal of discussion, and many law schools have recently been experimenting with new kinds of classes that focus on the practical challenges of lawyering and the challenges of building a professional identity.[3]

Where traditional classes ask you to sit and listen to a lecture, or answer a professor's questions about doctrine, most nontraditional classes aim to be more like law practice—which involves much more than answering questions about doctrine. Some of the classes I'm talking about—especially legal research and writing classes—have been part of the law school curriculum for a long time; I'm using the phrase "nontraditional class" to include any course that incorporates experiential learning and practical skills.

The most common kind of nontraditional class is the first-year course on legal research and writing, or "legal methods." The content of these classes varies dramatically from school to school. Some classes focus entirely on research and writing, while others also include other skills like oral argument. Your grade in these classes may be based on quizzes or exams that test your understanding of research techniques, or on an essay you research and write, or both. Some students treat legal writing courses as an annoyance—the least important part of the curriculum—but this is a mistake. Becoming a good writer is no less important, and no less challenging, than understanding the law of property or contract.

The most important opportunity to develop practical skills within the law school curriculum is in clinics. A clinic, as mentioned in chapter 1, is a sort of law practice operating within a law school. Students in clinics work for real clients, practicing law under the supervision of faculty members. Typically, students receive as much course credit for the clinic as they would for several traditional classes. The practical work you'll do in a clinic takes more time than a law school class, but on top of the hands-on work there is usually a teaching component: students meet regularly for training in the practical skills their work requires and to discuss what they've done and what they've learned. A cousin of the clinic is the *externship,* in which students receive course credit for working at a government office, a nonprofit organization, or—under certain circumstances—an off-campus law firm. There are also classes taught within the law school that focus on practical skills; particularly common are workshops on skills like trial advocacy, appellate advocacy, or negotiation.

It's reasonable to ask why you should use your limited time in law school to practice law or study practical skills, instead of taking traditional classes: you'll start practicing once you graduate anyway, so what's the hurry? One good answer is that in a well-run clinic, externship, or practical class, you spend time reflecting with the other students, and with your field or faculty supervisor on the work you're doing and the skills you're developing. As chapter 13 will explain, reflection of this kind is what makes it possible to develop good practical judgment, which every lawyer needs. Clinics give you the chance to reflect on your practical experience under the supervision of an experienced mentor—something that most jobs can't provide, because few practicing lawyers have time to hold detailed weekly reflection sessions for their mentees. The value of clinics and experiential learning is becoming widely accepted; law students at Yale can even begin taking clinics (and appearing in court) during their first year.[4]

Many professors and students underestimate the value of clinics and other practical classes, which is unfortunate.[5] Cognitive science and education theory strongly suggest that learning from "inside the problem situation" is qualitatively better than abstract learning.[6] As Gary Blasi writes, "It is not only that an engaged problem-solver learns *more* from both instruction and experience, but also that she learns something quite *different*."[7] Legal problems look different from the inside. It's one thing to talk about the death penalty; it's another thing entirely to represent a client who's facing it.[8] It's one thing to read about cross-examination. It's another thing to be forced to practice it, to try to ask a series of questions that will catch someone in a lie. It's one thing to criticize the way a legal text frames an issue; it's another thing to frame an issue on the fly, to pretend to be the lawyer arguing the case, and struggle to find the right words while a "judge" fires questions at you.

Some schools that uses what's called the problem method (as opposed to the "case method" used in traditional first-year classes). The problem method involves presenting students with a description of a challenging situation—often a situation in which a client wants advice on some difficult problem—and the lawyer has to figure out what law applies and what advice to give. Harvard students take a workshop during their first year that uses a version of the problem method in which students act out these situations: a professor pretends to be client, outlines a problem, and asks them for advice.[9]

The idea behind the problem method is to study law from the lawyer's perspective, rather than the judge's perspective. Other professors are exploring other ways of doing this. Even in traditional first-year classes, many professors are looking at ways to integrate real case documents into the reading and discussion, so that students can encounter facts and legal problems the way lawyers do.[10] The professors in your first-year core classes may use these, or other nontraditional methods; you may take a break from Socratic questioning for a simulated advice session, for example.

The problem method and simulation exercises aim to develop skills beyond the traditional legal-reasoning skills we've covered so far. The problem method is also useful because it looks a lot more like traditional exams—if you get some practice dealing with fact patterns during the year, they won't look quite so intimidating when you see them on exams.

Extracurricular Activities

Aside from classes, law schools offer a variety of extracurricular activities. There are moot courts, in which students play the role of lawyers arguing a case, or negotiating, or examining witnesses. There are also all kinds of clubs and advocacy groups. Some are purely social; at Harvard, there is In Vino Veritas, a wine-tasting society, and Beeritas, "the official Beer Appreciation Society of Harvard Law School." Others are devoted to particular subject interests, like the Environmental Law Society, or political orientations, like the American Constitution Society and the Federalist Society. Clubs can be a great source of information about jobs, and a way to make contacts in your field.

Other extracurricular activities involve more hands-on legal work. For example, there are groups like the Innocence Project, in which students work to exonerate wrongfully convicted prison inmates. The kind of work you do for a group like this can vary immensely, from reviewing trial transcripts and letters from inmates hoping to become the subject of an exoneration campaign to appearing in court. And there are lots of other opportunities to do real legal work for a good cause during law school; in fact, many law schools require students to do at least some pro bono work before graduation. ("Pro bono," by the way, is short for "pro bono publico," meaning "for the public good." Many lawyers think it means "for free," and although this isn't the literal meaning, you shouldn't call something "pro bono" if you get paid for it.)

The extracurricular activity that law students worry about the most is *law review*. Law reviews are the journals in which law professors publish their scholarly writing. In other academic fields, journals are typically edited by professors; in law school, students edit the vast majority of law reviews. Each law school has a "flagship" law review named after the school, which publishes articles on any legal subject, and one or more specialty law reviews, which focus on a specific subject area. For example, at the University of Alabama, the flagship law review is the *Alabama Law Review*, but there is also the *Journal of the Legal Profession*, which focuses on issues related to legal ethics and lawyering.

The members of law reviews are usually chosen through a "write-on" competition during the first year, in which students are given a week or so to write an essay on a specific topic, and those essays are used to choose who is offered a place on which law review. During the second year of law school, students who join law reviews typically do fairly routine editorial work, like proofreading and checking the citations for each article. In the third year, students typically take on more responsibility; one serves as editor-in-chief, and others help run the journal, interact with authors, and so on.

Law review work doesn't do much to develop the three skills traditional exams test. It won't help you distill the law, it won't help you learn to spot issues, and it won't do much to help you learn to argue. It does help develop your resume—for many employers, a law review on a resume is a shining gold star—and that might be reason enough to do it. But there are other reasons; law reviews can also help develop your legal writing skills, either by giving you practice editing other people's writing or just by teaching you to pay careful attention to detail. An eye for detail in writing is a skill that traditional law school classes don't develop much, but it matters a great deal in practice. I asked a judge once whether typos and citation mistakes in briefs really mattered. Of course they do, he said. If the lawyer hasn't checked the brief, I assume he's not checking the cases or the record either, so I read his briefs more suspiciously.

Law reviews may also give you an opportunity to publish a student Note (a short law review article). Publishing a Note is a great way to develop the ability to think seriously about a legal topic. If you intend to become a law professor, the importance of getting published early and often can't be overstated. But it's a good experience for anyone. Writing about law is a qualitatively better learning experience than reading about law.

Making Choices

How should you choose which extracurricular activities to get involved with, and which nontraditional classes to take? The number of options can feel overwhelming—and the activities themselves can be overwhelming if you take on more than you can handle. Many law students choose to stay away from extracurricular activities altogether during their first year, so they can concentrate on their course work, and for many this is a wise decision. But even if you do no extracurricular activities, you have to choose how much time to spend on your studying, and how many course credits to allocate to nontraditional classes.

Most of the book so far has been designed to help you see what it takes to do well on exams. But good grades aren't the only thing you'll need to prepare yourself for practice. And when you choose to spend your Wednesday afternoons studying, rather than volunteering for a group like

the Innocence Project, you're giving up an opportunity to prepare yourself for practice—and, potentially, an opportunity to cultivate skills that
prospective employers might value. It's important to understand not just
what's involved in getting good grades, but also what's involved in preparing yourself for practice. That's what the next part of the book is for.

What I am trying to write in fire on the wall is that the task before you is immense, is overwhelming, and that the official courses of the school are not enough to compass it.

KARL LLEWELLYN

PART IV
The Lawyer You'll Become

It would be nice if you could wait until the third year of law school to decide what kind of career you want to pursue, but that's not how it works. Halfway through your first year, you'll begin looking for your first summer job. From the day you enroll in law school, you'll have choices to make about whether to get involved with any number of extracurricular activities. You'll also have to decide whether to sign up for practice-oriented nontraditional classes; in some schools, those classes are available as early as the first year. The purpose of these classes, activities, and jobs is not—at least not primarily—to develop your legal-reasoning skills. It's to prepare you for practice in other ways. When you ask yourself whether it makes sense to invest time and energy in each of these things, the answer usually begins with "It depends on what kind of a career you want to pursue." So you need to start thinking early about where you're headed—what kind of career you want, and what kind of lawyer you want to become.

This part of the book tries to help you think about where you're headed. This means, first of all, thinking about what skills and abilities practicing lawyers need—what skills and abilities a prospective employer might be looking for. What choices can you make in law school that will show them you're developing those qualities?

A lawyer isn't a brain in a jar. When you apply for jobs, your prospective employers will want to know more than just whether you have good legal-reasoning skills. Legal-reasoning skills are important, but lawyers do more than think about legal doctrine. They investigate; they negotiate; they counsel; they perform oral arguments, examine witnesses, and analyze evidence. As Jerome Frank wrote many years ago, law students need to understand that "libraries and books are on the outer edge of matters law-yerlike, and that at the center is the conduct of human beings—clients, wit-nesses, judges, juries, legislative committees, stock market manipulators, labor leaders, presidents of corporations, farmers, and other lawyers."[1]

Your prospective employers will be looking to hire someone who'll do well in that world of "matters lawyerlike"—the real, human world of the law. But about 50 percent of practicing lawyers feel that law school didn't prepare them for their careers; and among those who do feel prepared, tra-ditional first-year classes are generally seen as the least relevant part of law school.[2] People who study legal education, too, are often critical of the way law school prepares students for practice. Sadly representative is one pro-fessor who wrote, "There is not a single lawyer I know with whom I went to law school who feels that his legal education adequately prepared him for the practice of law (or anything else for that matter)."[3] When you start an-swering questions in job interviews about whether you're ready to take on the responsibilities of a practicing lawyer, it would be nice to say something more hopeful than that about what law school has done to prepare you for practice. So you'll want to understand what makes someone ready to take on the responsibilities of a practicing lawyer. You'll want to know what skills and abilities you need to succeed in practice, so that you can choose which nontraditional classes and extracurricular activities to get involved with, and which summer jobs to apply for. Chapters 13 and 14 will explain some of these skills and abilities—some of the things prospective employers might be looking for when they decide whether you're the kind of law student who seems likely to turn into the kind of lawyer they want.

Of course, there are lots of different legal careers. You can't think about what qualities your prospective employers might be looking for unless you have some ideas about what kind of job you want. So chapters 15 and 16 talk about what you'll be deciding when you decide which jobs to pursue. Chapter 15 focuses on the kinds of roles you'll play in different jobs, and chapter 16 is about the professional identity you'll develop as you turn from layperson into lawyer.

> In the beginner's mind there are many possibilities; in the expert's mind there are few.

SHUNRYU SUZUKI

13 Judgment Calls

Sometime during your first year of law school, if all goes well, you'll sit down to begin a job interview, hoping that it will lead to your first summer job. You'll want to persuade the interviewers that you have good legal-reasoning skills. You'll also want them to think you're a likeable person. Beyond those basics, though, they'll be looking for another quality—the same quality that clients want to see in a lawyer they hire. They'll want to know whether you have good judgment.

How can you, as a first-year law student, give a prospective employer reason to believe that your judgment on the job will be good? You probably won't be able to talk about the tough practical lawyering decisions you've faced. Most law students don't have the opportunity to take a clinic in their first year, and many first-year students are too overwhelmed with class work to think about doing pro bono work. It would be nice to persuade the interviewer that you've somehow begun to develop good judgment in law school, even though you've never stepped into a courtroom or a law office. But where in law school can you develop good judgment?

Judgment as such doesn't form part of the traditional law school curriculum. Traditional classes—the ones that end in traditional exams—focus on legal-reasoning skills, not practical judgment. But this chapter will argue that it is possible to begin developing good practical judgment early in law school. There are two ways to do it. The first is to look for practice-oriented nontraditional classes and extracurricular activities like the ones described in chapter 12. These will give you experience making practical decisions— the kind of experiences that develop good judgment.

The second way to develop good judgment in law school is to practice reflecting on your experiences. As this chapter will explain, reflection on the situations you encounter, and the choices you make, is what
makes it possible to learn from experience—to develop good judgment.
And reflection is a skill you can begin to develop as soon as law school
begins.

But before we talk about how to develop good judgment, we should be
clear on what lawyers make judgments about. It's a surprisingly long list—
longer than you might infer from first-year classes, in which you focus
mostly on making judgments about law and legal texts. Lawyers do make
judgments about the law, of course. But when practicing lawyers interpret
legal texts, the judgments they make involve more than the kind of legal
reasoning you do in traditional law school classes. Practicing lawyers don't
just map out the arguments that could be made about legal texts; they have
to make predictions about how real decision makers (judges, juries, adver-
saries, ethical authorities, and so on) will interpret them. In classes, you
need only decide which arguments *could* be made. In practice, it's just as
important to predict which arguments will be made by your adversary and
accepted by the relevant decision makers.

Your first-year classes will focus on judgments about the law, but your
practice will require you to make judgments about many other things. For
example, lawyers make judgments about relationships. Most obviously,
there's the relationship with the client. How should you handle a situation
where you have to give a client bad news? How emotionally involved with
your client's case should you let yourself get? You'll make judgments about
other relationships too; litigators, for example, sometimes have to decide
whether to trust the other side to live up to a commitment, and your client
may depend on you to gauge the situation correctly.

Lawyers also make judgments about emotions. Lawyers who negotiate,
for example, have to decide how a certain concession will change the tone
of the debate. Everything can depend on this. Emotions are an important
part of decision making; it's a mistake to think of them as irrational and
irrelevant. They're part of how people reach conclusions about what to do
and what to think.

Lawyers also need to make judgments about strategy. Filing a lawsuit
might be a good way of accomplishing some goals, but a terrible way of accomplishing others. Lawyers also make judgments about goals themselves.
Say you're a divorce lawyer; your client's spouse is seeking a divorce. What's
your client's goal: to work things out, or to get as much of the marital property as possible? Your client isn't sure. How can you help? (Can you help at
all? Should you?)

Finally, lawyers make judgments about what's right. Say you're a criminal defense lawyer, or a student in a criminal defense clinic. The prosecutor offers your client a greatly reduced sentence if your client agrees to cooperate—by wearing a wire to incriminate his own brother. Your client is reluctant. "It's just wrong," he says. But then he says, "You're the lawyer, I'll do what you think is best." Many lawyers would prefer to say their job is just to tell the client what's in his interest—leave the moral questions to the client. But you know from experience that how you frame the choices for him may ultimately push him down one road or another. And the client wants your advice. Of course, it's in his interests to stay out of jail. But it's also in his interest to make a decision he can live with. What do you tell him?

Where do you get the resources to approach decisions like these? It seems obvious enough that good practical judgment is at least partly a product of practical experience. But it's worth asking exactly how experience builds judgment.

What Experience Is Made Of

First, let's examine the difference between an experienced practitioner—an expert—and a novice. When a novice doctor makes a diagnosis, she has to think through a long list of possibilities. She might use trial-and-error thinking to get to her conclusion: "Arthritis? No, arthritis alone wouldn't explain the rash." She might use mnemonic devices—remembering, for example, that a diagnosis of lupus requires four of the eleven symptoms whose initials are SOAP BRAIN MD,[1] and then running through that list in her head to see if it fits. An experienced doctor, on the other hand, might just look at the patient's chart, ask a few questions, and think, "Lupus." The expert doesn't need the mnemonic. She doesn't consider nearly as many possibilities. She "sees the problem all at once."[2]

What lets the experienced doctor see the problem all at once is the database of situations she has in her head.[3] She's encountered many challenging situations in her career, and made many decisions about what to do in each of them. Those situations and choices are stored away in her mind, forming a collection that she uses as a resource whenever she faces a new challenge. Her database also includes situations that she didn't personally face, but that she heard about from colleagues, or read about.

When an expert encounters a new problem, she tries to match the situation in front of her with a situation in her database. Sometimes they match exactly. Expert firefighters, for example, may need no internal debate about whether a burning house is about to collapse. Instead, they look around them and instantly recognize that the house is about to collapse.[4]

This quick intuition doesn't feel like a kind of reasoning; it feels more like recognition. An expert trial lawyer might see immediately that a new piece of information is something that must be disclosed to the court. In these flashes of recognition, the expert sees not just the problem, but also its solution. Your database of situations is also a database of solutions to the kinds of problems you've seen before.

But experience doesn't always lead to better judgment calls. In a recent study, researchers asked several hundred practicing lawyers to make predictions about their cases. A year later, the researchers asked how the cases had gone. Contrary to what you might expect, experience in practice didn't seem to make lawyers better at predicting the outcomes of their cases.[5] The seasoned lawyers were no better at prediction than the new lawyers. Why not? It's possible, the researchers noted, that experienced lawyers were handling more complicated cases. But it's also possible that experience itself was part of the problem.

Past experiences can box you into a particular way of thinking about things. If you've only made one kind of decision for your whole career, that's probably the only kind of decision you're going to be much good at. Your database of situations won't help you much if you only put one kind of situation into it. But the risk isn't just what you don't know; it's what you know too well. A lawyer who handles only one kind of case—only one kind of problem—learns to see everything in terms of the familiar framework. This is called "overlearning."[6] Gary Blasi says there's an old joke about it: some people have twenty years of experience, and some people have one year of experience twenty times.[7]

Imagine you're a client who thinks your employer has mistreated you. You have a choice between two lawyers. One has done nothing but litigation for twenty years. The other has done some litigation, but is also experienced with other approaches to dispute resolution, like negotiation, mediation, and arbitration. The first lawyer is likely to see the case only in terms of whether or not to sue, because she's spent twenty years seeing everything through that frame. The second lawyer, who knows other options, will be able to think about your case in a variety of ways. She'll be able to advise you about which framework might fit your case best because her database of situations has more possibilities in it.

An experienced lawyer can mistakenly put new problems into familiar boxes. To a person with a hammer, everything looks like a nail; to a lawyer whose entire practice consists of suing the daylights out of people, everything looks like a confrontation waiting to happen. Overlearning is a major risk that goes with experience—a way in which practical experience can *limit* a practitioner's judgment.

This is why judges are right to hire new lawyers, rather than experienced ones, as law clerks. Older and newer lawyers could both do a great job of legal research. But the new lawyers are in little danger of overlearning—they're able to question things that would appear unshakably obvious to someone whose mental habits were more fixed. Which is exactly what judges need: someone fresh enough not to think any question is too obvious or too stupid. A new law clerk's fresh, unstructured way of thinking can make her more likely to see questions that older lawyers would overlook.

To gain good judgment, you need to make sure that your experience doesn't lock you in to rigid structures that will prevent you from seeing new problems in all their uniqueness. How do you keep your judgment flexible? By having a wide variety of experiences, if possible. But equally important is learning to think well about your problems as you confront them—learning the skill of reflection.

Reflection Makes Experience Useful

Reflection is something that should be done both before and after a decision. By "reflection" I don't mean endless navel-gazing. Reflection usually involves pausing to step back from the problem in some way, but not necessarily for a long period of time. Different methods of reflection work best for different people; lawyers might use any number of strategies to reflect on a practical decision. They might make a list of pros and cons, or think step by step about what consequences would follow from each possible decision. They might ask, "What's our goal?" and reason backward from there. For many, reflection works best when it's a social process—a lawyer might talk to colleagues she respects about what they've done in similar situations, or ask colleagues to try to talk them out of the course of action they're leaning toward. Some strategies involve letting your subconscious mind take over for a little while—they might make a tentative decision, and then sleep on it. Any good strategy is going to involve some amount of conscious reflection; the number of possible strategies is vast.

There isn't always time for a detailed exploration of conscious decision-making strategies, but even a moment can be used well or poorly. One of the best lawyers I know has the habit of saying sometimes, during a meeting, "Wait a minute, let me think," and then pausing for a long, quiet moment to reflect before she explains what she's thinking. I don't know what she's doing in her head when she does this, but it's probably not the same thing I do in my head when I pause before a decision. Which strategy works best is itself something for you to reflect on.

Reflecting on a decision afterward is just as important as reflecting before you make it. That's how you learn from your experience. For example, one classic mistake in a Supreme Court argument is to ask a rhetorical question that draws a harsh response from a judge. As Supreme Court expert David Frederick writes, "Asking questions for their rhetorical effect . . . rarely works."[8] He uses this example from a real argument, in which a lawyer began his presentation with a rhetorical question:

[LAWYER]: Mr. Chief Justice, and may it please the Court: I think there's one thing everybody's missing, and that is, what is the problem? What is the problem with peaches, plums, and nectarines in California that's any different than the other 32 States that grow these commodities?

[JUSTICE SCALIA]: Disorderly markets are the problem.[9]

Which completely derailed the lawyer's argument; apparently he wasn't prepared for this answer. Before the lawyer could make any affirmative points, Frederick writes, the lawyer had "already been knocked off track by his own rhetorical question."[10]

A good lawyer will reflect on an experience like this later. She might think, *Something went terribly wrong in my opening.* As she replays the experience in her mind, she'll identify the moment when things went wrong: *It was when I asked that rhetorical question. That let Justice Scalia jump in with a sarcastic response that wrecked my momentum.* And so in the future, she'll shy away from asking rhetorical questions, a new and helpful reflex.

If she keeps reflecting, she may draw a deeper lesson: *Be very careful about provoking questions from judges.* When she plans her next argument, she'll think about what kinds of questions each point might provoke. The deeper principle she's exploring is *be aware of your audience.* But just telling someone *be aware of your audience* doesn't always help much. A direct experience of the ways in which misjudging your audience can ruin your argument, on the other hand, is priceless. So a single bad experience can lead a lawyer to a new level of sophisticated judgment about her practice, because she reflected on it well.

A different lawyer might walk out of an argument like this and think *Good lord, the justices were really tough on me*—and never take his reflections further. It might be perfectly true that the justices were tough, but knowing that won't help with the next argument. In fact, it may make the lawyer's next argument worse, because he's wrongly concluded that the judges are arbitrary and mean, which will make it much harder for him to communicate with them next time.

The valuable lessons you learn aren't propositions you distill from your experience, like *be aware of your audience*. Those are too general. They're habits you develop, behaviors you learn, ways of thinking you cultivate. In your next oral argument, you'll shy away from the rhetorical question because you automatically recognize it as a bad idea, with your new and hard-earned intuition. That hard-earned intuition, though, is made possible by the process of reflecting *consciously* on your experiences. The ultimate lessons are not the kind of knowledge that can be put into words. But you won't learn them unless you think consciously about what worked and what didn't.

Law students, just like practicing lawyers, can get a lot out of reflecting on decisions after they make them. Just as the Supreme Court practitioner could have walked away from an unpleasant exchange with a valuable lesson or with a vague sense of having been beaten up on, a law student who speaks up in class can walk away with a more or less useful understanding of what happened.

If you get into an exchange with your professor in class, it's useful to reflect afterward on how it went. The point is not to decide whether you did well or poorly; it's to think about what you learned from the experience. For example, did the professor seem frustrated when you shied away from taking a strong position? Why? Think about how you felt, too—about what aspects of the conversation felt more or less comfortable to you. There are all kinds of lessons that can be drawn from an experience of speaking in class. The more thoughtfully you reflect on your experience, the more likely it is that you'll draw useful lessons, like "It seems to work best when I begin by stating my conclusion"—rather than less useful lessons like "Wow, that made my brain hurt."

Similarly, after you take an exam, reflect on what went well and what didn't. You might notice, for example, that by the time you started the last question, you felt so mentally exhausted that it was hard to keep your thoughts straight. So next time, maybe you'll begin by outlining all the questions while your brain is still fresh. Reflection like this is not just daydreaming; it's work. It's something you have to sit down and make yourself do. It's how you learn from your experience.

None of this should be taken to imply that reflection can guarantee good judgment. The judgments we make, whether we're experts or novices, are vulnerable to all kinds of biases and distorting effects, and psychologists in recent decades have been having a rollicking good time identifying them.

People are more likely to be dishonest, for example, when they're wearing sunglasses.[11] When people are asked to volunteer for Habitat for Humanity, they're more likely to say yes if they're in a room that's recently been sprayed with citrus-scented Windex.[12] And people make harsher moral judgments when they are exposed to the smell of farts.[13]

Nor can expertise guarantee sound intuitions. A study of parole board hearings in Israel, for example, found that the judges granted parole much more often when they'd recently taken a break to eat. The percentage of favorable rulings dropped from about 65 percent right after a meal break to almost zero by the end of the session, and then returned abruptly to about 65 percent after the next break.[14]

All of this has important implications for new lawyers. When you encounter a professor or a practicing lawyer who seems very sure of something, remember that experts' intuitions aren't always the product of their expertise. It's possible they're falling victim to a bias. Whether you're an expert or a novice, some of your intuitions shouldn't be trusted.

What can you do about these biases? You can learn about them; Daniel Kahneman's book *Thinking, Fast and Slow* is a great place to start. But research hasn't yet produced much evidence that learning about cognitive biases can help you avoid them. Learning about biases does seem to help you predict other people's behavior.[15] And that can be very helpful—if you're on one side of a lawsuit, it's important to understand what affects your adversary's judgment. But people who learn about cognitive biases tend to doubt their own judgment will be affected by them. In fact, the average person believes herself to be significantly less subject to cognitive biases than the average person.[16]

So mistakes and misjudgments are inevitable, whether you're a novice or a beginner. But mistakes can be an important part of your database of situations—as long as you reflect thoughtfully on them. The lawyer whose argument was derailed by a rhetorical question had a chance to learn several valuable lessons about oral argument tactics and the importance of paying attention to his audience. When you identify and acknowledge your mistakes, you make it easier to avoid making them again.

The same thing is true in law school. Even if you're committed to reflection, you'll still make mistakes—you'll say things in class that sound wrong in retrospect; you'll misunderstand some of the cases you read; and you'll miss important issues on exams. Mistakes are inevitable—even if there were no cognitive biases or situational pressures, people are fallible. The question is whether you'll turn the mistakes into something useful. Reflection won't stop you from making mistakes, but mistakes can be more than just a reason for regret. If you do the work of reflecting on them, they can be important parts of your database of situations.

Learning to Reflect

There are opportunities in law school to gain practical experience, and opportunities to experiment with the best ways to reflect on your experience. But you have to know what you're looking for.

Traditional law school classes don't offer you much in the way of practical experience—you don't work with clients, and the cases you think about are long since over, and summed up for you in your casebooks. But that doesn't mean that traditional classes contribute nothing. The experience of speaking in class—engaging with professors—is just as real, and sometimes just as challenging, as the experiences you'll have in practice. Much of the "real-world" experience that awaits you in law practice involves conversations of one kind or another, because conversations are a big part of what most lawyers do. So engaging with your professor in a challenging conversation really is preparation for practice. If you become the kind of lawyer who appears in court, you may find that someday, when you're being grilled by a judge, you remember some of the lessons you learned while being grilled by professors in law school.

That's assuming, of course, that you did learn something from being grilled in traditional classes. Reflection on your experience—the key to getting something useful out of it—isn't really part of most traditional classes. Unlike clinics, in which the students meet regularly to discuss their experiences and reflect on them, the professors in traditional classes don't usually pause to reflect on the experience of speaking in class and what students are learning from it. So reflecting on that experience is up to you.

There are lots of opportunities to get practical experience and reflect on it in the nontraditional classes and extracurricular activities discussed in chapter 12. Clinics and practical experience are an increasingly normal part of law school. About a third of law students today participate in at least one clinic, and another third participate in a field placement of some kind, so only a third of law students graduate with no experience in practice.[17] New lawyers report that clinics are significantly more helpful than any other part of the law school curriculum in making the transition to the work they do as lawyers.[18]

When you decide whether to enroll in clinics or other practical courses, and when you decide which extracurricular activities to get involved in, it's important to think not only about the experience you'll be getting, but also about what kind of reflection you'll be doing. Clinics usually offer the best opportunities to develop the skill of reflection, because they approach it from so many angles. You'll often have a partner—another law student— with whom you discuss each practical decision you make. Typically, the clinic students also meet regularly as a group for a discussion of their experiences. And the professors often assign some background reading on whatever practical task you're doing—like reading on how to interview a traumatized client, or how to present an oral argument in court. Each of these perspectives gives the students a little more information to put into their database of situations.

It's a good idea to think about any clinic, nontraditional class, or extracurricular activity not just in terms of the experience it'll give you, but also in terms of the opportunities for developing reflection strategies. In some externships, for example, you'll be working off campus for busy lawyers who may not make an effort to sit down with you to reflect on your work. And in some extracurricular activities there may not be much group interaction at all. At some law reviews, many of the student editors do little more than cite checking—the senior editor will e-mail them a portion of an article, and ask them to look up each of the sources it cites to make sure they're correctly cited, and that's pretty much the whole job. There's no reflection apart from the reflection you do on your own, so you'll need to experiment, and learn what type of reflection works best for you.

In other activities, like some of the pro bono projects that involve working directly with clients, there may be extensive supervision and work with faculty mentors. Those relationships are great opportunities to develop your reflection skills—and, of course, to develop relationships with faculty members that may turn out to be useful in all sorts of ways. Whichever activity you choose, it's worth asking whether it will help you get better at reflection.

Some people are skeptical of the value of clinics and other practical classes because they think you learn by doing, not by thinking and talking about the things you do. But the habit of reflecting on experience is one of the main things that distinguishes effective professionals from ineffective ones. It's not hard to see why. Imagine two baseball players, equally talented. One has a coach, one doesn't. Who gets better faster? Right.

Now that you understand what good judgment is made of—a database of situations you've experienced, and the skill of reflection—you'll be much better equipped to make choices about which courses and activities will help your judgment. You'll also be better equipped to answer the question we started the chapter with—how you, as a law student with little experience, can persuade a prospective employer that you'll make good practical decisions on the job. It's great to tell stories about judgment calls you've made while working in a clinic, or some other experiential-learning class if you have them. But if not, you have the opportunity to display the skill of reflecting well when you answer interview questions.

Say, for example, that the interviewer asks what your favorite class was. This is a chance to show that you've thought about the lessons you're learning from your experience in class. Here's one possible answer: "I loved torts because of all those crazy fact patterns. Especially the case where two hunters happened to fire their guns at the plaintiff at the same time, and nobody could tell whose pellet was stuck in his eye."[19] This is perfectly good small talk, but it doesn't say much about your judgment. Here's another answer: "I liked torts because the professor had a way of asking questions that made you feel like the ground was being yanked out from under you. And once you've had that happen to you a few times, you learn not to panic. I thought that was a really valuable lesson." The second answer shows thoughtful reflection on the process of becoming a lawyer; it gives the interviewer reason to think that the student will grow and learn with each practical judgment she makes. There are few better reasons to hire someone than that.

[T]he things we have to learn before we can do, we learn by doing.

ARISTOTLE

14   What Lawyers Do

One kind of question you might be asked in a job interview has to do with your skills. Along with the other things a prospective employer might be looking for—legal-reasoning skills, good practical judgment, and an appealing personality—there are specific skills that most lawyers need. This chapter focuses on four of them: writing, speaking, dispute resolution, and research. Almost every legal job will call on these skills at some point or another. That's not to say they're the only skills a lawyer might need—far from it. There are so many different kinds of lawyering jobs, dealing with so many different fields of human activity, that a list of the skills that might come in handy would be endless. For a lawyer who represents scientists applying for patents, it might be scientific reasoning skills; for a lawyer who works on corporate mergers, it might be accounting; for a personal injury lawyer, it might be the marketing and promotion skills required to attract a steady stream of clients. But the four skills covered in this chapter are skills that all lawyers are likely to need, in one form or another, over the course of their careers. They're also the skills that just about any prospective employer might be looking for. This chapter will give you some ideas about what the skills are, and where in law school you might go to develop them.

Writing

Most lawyers spend a lot of time writing. They write in a range of ways, from the most formal (contracts or statutes) to the most informal (dashed-off e-mails).

Lawyers write for many reasons. They write to persuade when they draft a legal brief on behalf of a client. They write to inform when they write a memo to colleagues giving background for an upcoming decision. They also write the law itself—statutes, judicial opinions, regulations, and so on—and the documents that govern people's rights and entitlements, like contracts, wills, and deeds. Some lawyers even write for pleasure. Each of the basic kinds of jobs lawyers do—advocating before a tribunal, advising clients, and so on—frequently requires that lawyers do their work in writing.

Learning to write well takes time, but it's worth it. Lawyers who represent clients need to write well; a lawyer who writes the client a memo explaining the law needs to be sure that the client will understand what she's written. A deeper reason to spend time on your writing is that learning to write clearly is learning to think clearly. There's a well-known phenomenon among judges who write opinions in difficult cases: Sometimes, a judge whose mind is made up will sit down to write an opinion that explains her position, but as she puts her thoughts into written words, she just can't get the opinion down on paper in a way that satisfies her. She changes her decision, and drafts a new opinion ruling for the other side.

Judges who have this experience sometimes say that the first opinion they tried to draft "just wouldn't write." The phrase implies that the opinion was writing itself, and the judge was merely observing. In a sense, that's how writing works. The writer sees her ideas from a distance when she puts them into writing. Writing allows you to step back from your thoughts and see them as a stranger would. It makes reflection much easier. In fact, it can be difficult to reflect on your ideas well without putting them into writing.

Your writing style matters, because it's part of your professional identity. Much legal writing is awful, because lawyers fall thoughtlessly into the tired conventions of legalese. The last chapter talked about how bad judgment can get locked in over the years. This is particularly true of the judgments we make about writing. Many lawyers seem to believe their writing will sound more professional if they use clotted jargon like "hereinafter" and "the above-captioned matter." They pick up these bad habits from what they read: the judicial opinions and other legal documents that collectively teach us what legal language is supposed to sound like. The pressure these materials exert on new lawyers is obviously intense. How else but through intense social pressure could anyone get the idea that when you mention a number you should use words and numerals—as in, "three hundred (300) dollars." Does anyone think the phrase "three hundred" is ambiguous? To avoid the slide into jargon and banality, you'll have to pay attention to your writing as writing. That's a worthy project, and one that will make you not just a better writer but a clearer thinker too.

Legal writing is taught in law schools. First-year classes on legal research and writing will give you the basics of what a legal document looks like: you'll draft a memo or a brief, and learn some of the basic forms of legal writing. Later, you'll take a class that requires you to write a research paper. But these are just beginnings; learning to write well takes years of practice and reflection.

It also takes years of reading. As Richard Posner says, "Occasional reading of literature will not alter the neural circuits involved in writing"; the only way to write well is to immerse yourself in good writing.[1] Most of what you learn about writing is learned from what you read. Unfortunately, the cases you read are often terribly written. Here's how Judge Posner summarizes the implicit lessons about writing that await you in your casebooks: "Make your sentences long"; "Be euphemistic"; "Sound old."[2] Some of the opinions are written in a grand style that you'd be ill-advised to emulate. Others are written in the gray, obscure language of the modern bureaucrat. Only a few are well written. Most law school classes don't dwell on how the judge expressed what needed to be said. So if you want to become a good writer, you'll have to do more than law school asks.

You'll also have to reflect on your writing experiences. Think about what works well. Talk about it. If you're fortunate, you'll have mentors who take writing seriously. But what matters most is that you yourself read. For help reflecting on your writing, there are some wonderful books aimed specifically at lawyers, some of which are discussed in "Suggestions for Further Reading" at the back of this book. Posner warns you about handbooks, writing that "following handbooks of style, while it will correct the worst habits of bad writers, will leave their writing lifeless."[3] But that depends on how you use the handbooks. If you just *follow* them—avoiding the mistakes they point out, accepting their advice without question—it's true that your own writing won't benefit much. But if you use them as catalysts for reflection on your writing, they can help start the process that is most essential to your development as a writer.

Speaking

Lawyers speak to courts, to clients, and to other lawyers. In some situations, they speak formally, like when they address a judge, and in other situations they speak informally, like when they brainstorm with colleagues. In some situations, they speak for public consumption, and in others they speak about intimately private matters. Sometimes lawyers speak about highly technical, complex questions of law or business or science, and sometimes they speak about ordinary things in plain English.

Lawyers speak for different reasons. Sometimes the reason for speaking is to persuade, like when lawyers speak to judges about their clients' legal positions. Persuasive speech is a tricky business; it can be difficult to balance the need to aggressively assert your interpretation of the law (or the facts) and the need to maintain your credibility.

Sometimes the reason for speaking is to provide information to others, like when lawyers explain legal rules to clients. In some situations—closing arguments at trial, lectures, speeches, presentations at meetings—a lawyer must develop an idea of her own, at some length, which requires learning to structure a spoken presentation.

In many situations, lawyers need to go beyond just telling the client how things are; when the client wants advice (rather than just an explanation of the law), another mode of speech—counseling—is called for. Counseling involves helping clients make difficult decisions by giving them advice about what to do. Lawyers counsel clients on major life decisions, or advise corporations about business choices. Counseling is a sensitive and difficult process; there are books on it.[4]

Another reason for speaking is to get information. Lawyers need to know how to ask questions of all kinds—questions about facts, questions about law, and questions about what people want, feel, and believe. Sometimes the person being questioned wants to share information—clients are usually, though not always, cooperative questionees—but lawyers may also have to get information from people who don't want them to have it. It takes years to learn to frame questions well.

Keep in mind that speaking skills can't be developed without other skills that make them possible. Every situation that requires you to speak also requires you to *listen*. Good appellate advocates, good interviewers, good supervisors, and good negotiators are distinguished by their ability to listen, attentively and insightfully, to their judges, witnesses, supervisees, and interlocutors. Almost all legal speech is conversation. And listening skills are only part of the broad category of interpersonal skills that make it possible to communicate well. Others include tact, likability, patience, and the ability to set people at ease. To varying degrees, each of these skills—even likability—can be learned, and taught, and each of them can be developed by people who pay attention to what they're doing and whether it works.

Law students have several opportunities to develop their professional speaking skills. Among the most important opportunities are the informal conversations that you'll have with classmates about the law. In law practice, informal conversations about law are an important tool lawyers use to understand the law and the problems they face. One of the best ways to ensure a good decision is to find colleagues with good judgment and talk the problem through with them. Informal conversations in law school—study groups, for example—are a chance to get good at this kind of conversation. The more you experience situations in which you've talked through a problem with colleagues, the better you'll be at group thinking. As with all kinds of learning, this will work better if you reflect on how it's going. After a study group, think—or talk—about what worked and what didn't. If you came to the group with a doctrine you didn't understand, and a conversation helped you make sense of it, why? What worked? If it didn't work, why not?

Traditional classes are another opportunity to develop professional speaking skills. In traditional classes, when you answer the professor's questions and try to articulate an understanding of the law, you're learning to present information under pressure. You're also learning to speak persuasively—to defend a position well. As chapter 8 explained, classes can be a great opportunity to experience a certain kind of legal conversation, and to reflect on it.

But traditional classes rarely include any explicit reflection on speaking skills. The only piece of advice I got about how to speak like a lawyer in my traditional classes was—this is an ancient piece of law school wisdom—"Be crisp." I have nothing against the idea of crispness, except that it tends to make me compare myself unfavorably to iceberg lettuce. But you may have to look beyond traditional classes to develop your question-framing skills, your advice-giving skills, and your listening skills. The nontraditional classes and extracurricular activities discussed in chapter 12 can give you lots of opportunities to develop these skills. Clinics, for example, can give you the chance to speak in many different legal situations, from formal speech in courts to witness interviewing to brainstorming with colleagues. Importantly, clinics also give you the chance to reflect on the speaking you've done, and what went well, and to learn from your colleagues' experiences too.

The same is true of classes on negotiation and alternative dispute resolution. ("Alternative dispute resolution" refers to ways of settling disputes without litigation, like mediation or arbitration.) These classes are usually experiential, because the general view among negotiation teachers is that learning about negotiation requires doing it, and then reflecting on the experience. Negotiation classes typically involve simulated negotiation—but simulated negotiation is real communication. The opportunity to reflect on the particular challenges involved in negotiations and dispute resolution situations is extremely valuable, as the next section will discuss.

There are also moot courts and mock-trial events, at which you can work on your formal legal speech. These are great opportunities, particularly if your mock-trial team makes a practice of critiquing members' performance. If you're not going to spend any time debriefing and reflecting, the experience will still be useful, but less so.

Finally, don't underestimate the value of going to speak to professors during their office hours. Speaking to professors about the law is similar to a number of situations lawyers encounter. It's a bit like speaking to a judge, and a bit like speaking to another lawyer, and a bit like brainstorming with colleagues. It's casual speech about the law with an extremely well-informed person. If your professors make you nervous, that makes it all the more valuable to speak to them informally. Practicing lawyers often have to have conversations about the law with people who, for one reason or another, make them nervous—a supervisor, a judge, a prospective client. It's not always easy to be a good listener when you're nervous. And it can be hard to say "I still don't understand" to someone you'd like to impress. But these are crucial skills in law practice (especially the ability to say "I don't know"!), and your professors' office hours can be a great opportunity to cultivate them.

Negotiation and Dispute Resolution

Lawyers often find themselves in situations that require dispute resolution skills. In fact, it might be said that the lawyer's most basic job is to resolve disputes (although, admittedly, some lawyers do more to start disputes than to resolve them). Trials are a form of dispute resolution, the form that traditional law school classes focus on. But they're an expensive and risky way of settling disputes, which is why the vast majority of civil lawsuits are resolved by settlements—negotiated agreements—before the trial process reaches a conclusion.

There are a growing number of alternatives to trials. The field of alternative dispute resolution, often called "ADR," is an increasingly important part of legal studies. Rather than going to trial, parties in disputes can choose from a number of alternatives to trials. In *arbitration*, the adjudicator's ruling is binding, like a judge's, but she is hired by the parties, rather than the justice system, and is often an expert in the relevant substantive area. *Mediation* involves a privately hired facilitator who has no power to bind the parties, but who may be able to help them reach an agreement. There are also a number of hybrid mechanisms for formal dispute resolution, including one with the unpleasant name "med-arb."

Some negotiations may take place with no neutral third party; lawyers frequently negotiate directly with each other. Lawyers often encounter situations that call for informal dispute resolution, including disputes that can arise in the lawyer's own workplace. Each of these situations calls for a variety of skills: the judgment and research skills involved in planning the negotiation; the interpersonal and communication skills involved in conducting the negotiation; the judgment skills involved in deciding when to continue a negotiation and when to break it off.

Practicing lawyers increasingly cite negotiation and dispute-resolution skills as among the most important skills lawyers need.[5] And dispute resolution is one of the fastest-growing areas of research in the legal academy. There is a growing body of theoretical and popular literature on what works well in negotiations and what doesn't. And so there's a large body of literature on negotiation and dispute-resolution skills available to lawyers who want to understand those skills better. Many law schools now offer classes in negotiation and ADR. These classes can be an excellent opportunity. Most of them combine the theory of negotiation with practical role-playing exercises. Students learn about negotiation, then try it, then reflect on their experience in a conversation facilitated by an expert. That process—of study followed by experience followed by reflection—is probably the best possible scenario for learning anything, and the chance to practice the skill of reflection is itself a great reason to take a class on negotiation.

There are other ways to learn negotiation and dispute resolution skills in law school. A clinic or externship may involve you in an actual negotiation on behalf of a real client. Some law schools have negotiation competitions modeled on moot court competitions, in which students pit their skills against others. Many other activities involve negotiation of one kind or another; study groups, for example, inevitably spend time negotiating what they'll be working on. On some level, any conversation involves an element of negotiation, even if it's only a negotiation about the terms of the conversation itself. In fact, one of the best reasons to take a negotiation class is that if you're a person who finds the idea of negotiation intimidating, the class will help you see how much negotiating you've been doing every day of your life.

Research

So far we've been talking the output of lawyers' work, which is communication—written or oral. (That's what lawyers make: words.) The *input* of lawyers' work is information. The situations lawyers encounter require them to find two kinds of information: facts and legal texts.

Finding legal texts is a pretty narrow set of skills: you must know how to use Westlaw and/or Lexis; you should know the location of the nearest library for access to the books that aren't available through those databases; and for more unusual sources, like treaties or state legislative history materials, you'll sometimes have to get creative.

Finding facts is much more complicated. As Jerome Frank wrote, "the actual facts in a suit do not walk into the courtroom," and uncertainty about the facts can be a life-and-death matter.[6] There are formal fact-finding methods that are part of the civil litigation process, like discovery (in which the parties are required to turn over relevant information to each other) and depositions (a part of discovery in which each side gets to interview potential witnesses on the record). Each of these require a particular set of communication skills, as well as (of course) good judgment.

Informal fact finding—detective work—can involve anything from what a friend of mine calls "a little light Googling" to meeting confidential informants in dark parking garages. Investigations are a central part of many lawyers' practice. Corporate lawyers conduct internal investigations of accounting practices; prosecutors help run criminal investigations; civil rights lawyers investigate patterns of discrimination. These are extremely important kinds of lawyers' work. But it's unlikely you'll learn much about them in law school.

Finding legal texts—the skill of legal research—is usually taught in first-year classes on legal methods. You'll get a basic introduction to the available sources. But you can get through most law schools without developing much skill in legal research, because in most of your classes the materials you need are packaged up neatly in your casebooks. The exception, of course, is clinics, where you'll need to conduct legal research with the same urgency and under the same time pressures you will in practice.

Formal fact finding—discovery—can be studied in some law school classes; civil procedure classes usually include an introduction to the rules governing discovery. But knowing the rules won't make you good at discovery, any more than knowing the rules of chess will make you a good player.

The opportunities to learn about informal fact finding in law school come mostly in clinics and projects that involve representing real clients, because whenever you have a real client you have an obligation to find out what's going on in the world. In a criminal defense clinic, you might go knocking on doors looking for witnesses to a shooting. In an asylum clinic, you might call government offices in Africa looking for evidence that your client once passed through a particular city. In a family law clinic, you might interview a child about the way her foster parents treated her. All of these are very useful experiences—especially because in clinics, you'll be debriefed on them by professors, and talk the experiences over with colleagues, which will help you make sense of them. Some extracurricular clubs can also help develop fact-finding skills. In particular, there's the Innocence Project and groups like it, which look for evidence that convicted prisoners are innocent.

For each of these skills—speaking, writing, negotiating, and research-ing—learning works best when it's accompanied by reflection. To learn to speak, to write, to negotiate, or to research well, try to find teachers and colleagues who'll help you reflect on your work. That's how you'll learn which questions to ask.

Once I asked a broker what he loved
about his job, and he said *Making a killing*.
Once I asked a serial killer what made him
get up in the morning, and he said *The people*.

SANDRA BEASLEY, "Vocation"

15 The Hats Lawyers Wear

When you make decisions about whether to pursue extracurricular activities and nontraditional classes, you'll want to bear in mind what kind of a career they'll help you move toward. But this, for many law students, is a daunting prospect: in your first year, when you're still so new to the law, how could you know much about what kind of legal job you want to pursue? It's not an abstract question; you'll be applying for your first summer job halfway through your first year, and first summer jobs can have a big influence on where you end up working. Law students have dramatically different experiences on the job market; some have many choices, and some have few or none. But even if your choices are limited, it's important to be clear on what your goals are.

This chapter argues that you should think of your choice of jobs in terms of a choice of roles. By "role" I mean not just the kind of job a lawyer has, but all of the behaviors that are expected from her in that job. Your role isn't who you are, exactly; it's more like who everyone else expects you to be. The roles that different kinds of lawyers inhabit—the ways they're expected to behave—are very different. Major categories of lawyerly role include advocate, counselor, negotiator, facilitator, independent investigator, and scholar. Within each category there are lots of subspecies. To say that many lawyers play the role of counselor, for example, sweeps together a huge variety of subspecies within that role. People expect very different kinds of behavior from small-town family lawyers who counsel clients through major life decisions and big-city lawyers who advise developers and investors on massive real estate deals.

Not that conformity to others' expectations is always the best strategy. Some of the best movies about lawyers are fish-out-of-water stories in which the lawyer just won't act the way people expect, like *Legally Blonde* and *My Cousin Vinny*. And the movies are right: roles aren't straitjackets, and sometimes it's best to struggle against them. But your experience will be profoundly shaped by people's expectations about the role you play.

Each kind of role offers different kinds of satisfactions. A commercial litigator's good day looks very different from a criminal defense lawyer's good day. One way to think about what role you want for yourself is to think about what *your* good day looks like. If your biggest thrill is victory over an adversary, that suggests a certain kind of lawyering role. If your good day is one that includes a satisfying conversation with a colleague about a thorny intellectual problem, that suggests another kind of lawyering role.

It's important to keep an open mind. You might make a choice early on, and discover with time that you were wrong—that the role that suits you best is one you never expected to love. Your attitudes and beliefs about your role will be subject to constant revision throughout your career. It's not easy to find the right job. That's why it's important to be in the habit of reflecting on how things are going.

Lawyering Roles

There are lots of ways to divide up the world of possible lawyering roles. The distinction most students start with is *private practice* versus *public interest.* The stereotype is that lawyers in private practice make more money, and lawyers in government or the nonprofit sector get to spend more time with their families. There's some truth in that. When law is a business, the incentives change. But it's important not to oversimplify.

Consider, for example, one feature of private practice: the billable hour, the dominant pay structure in for-profit law firms. Almost half of lawyers in private practice bill 1,900 hours each year, which means sixty-hour work weeks.[1] For obvious reasons, billable-hours requirements are much loathed; Geoffrey Hazard writes that no profession can get "serious mental effort out of its members at the rate of 2,000 hours per year."[2]

But, again, be careful of generalizations. Not all private practitioners suffocate under the weight of the billable hour. There's a world of difference between 1,700 billable hours per year (which is not unusual in some smaller cities), and 2,200 billable hours (which you might find at some big-name firms). Twenty-two hundred billable hours, you might suspect, would require an almost cultish commitment to the firm and a renunciation of virtually all family and social ties. Maybe so. But those kinds of demands are not universal in the world of private practice.

It's also true that in private practice there's an imperative to bring in new business. But here, too, it's important not to oversimplify: not all private practice lawyers are schmoozers who hang around cocktail parties or emergency rooms looking for leads. Some very successful lawyers generate business by specializing in a particular area of law and developing a reputation for being good at it.

As for the money: on average, a lawyer in private practice makes more money than a lawyer in public interest. And money is a serious matter. The average law student now graduates with $150,000 in student-loan debt, not including undergraduate debt.[3] But here, again, be wary of generalizations: some public interest lawyers and government lawyers make a good deal of money. And most lawyers in private practice don't make anything like the huge salaries that Wall Street firms offer.

It's important, by the way, not to assume you can't afford to work in public interest. Many law students cite student-loan burdens as a reason for not choosing public interest work.[4] But there are loan-repayment programs available to many students who go into public interest work, both from law schools and from the federal government. (Ask your career-services office to show you how they work.) That said, it's undoubtedly true that many students aren't able to get enough help with their loans. And prestigious law firms do pay a lot more.

The satisfactions you find vary too. If you ask lawyers in private practice to identify the most rewarding part of their job, some will tell you it's the relationships they form with the client—the bonds of trust and even friendship that define their work. But of course that's not confined to private practice: many public interest lawyers do direct-services work, providing legal help to people who can't afford it—they too have that lawyer-client relationship. On the other hand, many lawyers in private practice, especially at big firms, represent institutions. When you're a new associate for a big firm representing a big corporation, you may never meet the people you're working for—and if you did, they'd just be lawyers (in-house counsel) who work for the company. The lawyer-client bond is, for many people, the point of lawyering, but nobody has a monopoly on it.

Phil Schrag argues that public interest lawyers get more interesting work, as a simple matter of necessity. Nonprofit organizations are understaffed, he says, so there's no choice but to give lots of responsibility to new lawyers.[5] That's probably true; you rarely hear young public interest lawyers complaining about the menial document review they've been assigned. But, once again, be careful. Nobody has more responsibility than a young solo practitioner entrusted with a difficult issue. All of these generalizations are just generalizations; to make a good decision, you'll have to look deeper. There are differences between private practice and public interest in general, but what matters is where *you* end up, not what the lawyering landscape looks like from space.

WHAT YOU'RE WORKING FOR

The distinction between public interest and private practice is often an imprecise way of getting at the question of what your work is *for*. I don't mean your organization's mission statement or bylaws; I mean your sense of what matters about your job.

In public interest law practice, for example, there's a distinction between *direct services*, in which you represent clients who are impoverished or otherwise unable to obtain legal services through the free market, and *impact litigation*, in which you represent clients chosen not because they are in need of services, but because their case represents an opportunity to establish a particular principle. (Public defenders do direct-services work; the ACLU does impact litigation.) The purpose of the direct-services lawyer's work is to fill the client's need; the purpose of the impact litigator's work is to further a social policy.

A similar distinction creeps into private practice. Some firms develop institutional identities that are bound up with particular kinds of work. For example, there are firms that specialize in plaintiff-side labor law: they only bring lawsuits on behalf of employees who feel wronged by their employers. These firms are for-profit, but their purpose is similar to the impact litigator's. Certain firms are seen as defendants' firms or plaintiffs' firms in particular kinds of cases. The "hired gun" metaphor—the lawyer who will take any case—is too simple for some parts of the world of private practice. Firms sometimes do have a sense of mission, and it's worth considering what that mission is, and how it suits you.

Of course, many lawyers reject the idea of a mission altogether. They say that the rewards of lawyering are in the work, not the results. Chief Justice Roberts testified in his confirmation hearings that although he had helped lawyers prepare to argue in favor of gay rights in *Lawrence v. Texas*, he would have just as willingly helped the lawyers for the other side if they'd come to him first. For Roberts, the rewards of lawyering had little to do with which side the lawyering was *for*. He said that his willingness to work on either side of an issue was because of what he saw as the real reward of lawyering: the experience of "serv[ing] the rule of law, above and beyond representing particular clients."[6] The question for you is where you'll find your rewards.

THE CLIENT

Another thing to consider is whether you want to have clients at all. Some lawyers' roles are centered on the client. Some lawyers really don't have clients; prosecutors, for example, technically represent "the people," but in practice there is no one outside the prosecutor's office to whom they report. Other lawyers have clients that are corporations or other non-corporeal entities. When you represent a corporation, you never meet your client because it lacks a physical body and can't walk into meetings. Instead, you meet other people who, like you, are agents of your client: corporate officers, or (more often) lawyers who work on the corporation's payroll.

For some lawyers, what makes law practice worthwhile is the living, breathing client who walks into your office and needs your help. For others, the client is the only thing standing in the way of an enjoyable day. It's hard to know in advance which category you'll fall into.

WHAT YOU DO ALL DAY

You might think about your career choice in terms of the *activities* a given role will require—what you'll do all day. Do you want to be a lawyer who appears in court (a litigator), or a lawyer who drafts agreements and other legal documents (a transactional lawyer)?

It's important to think about your role in terms of how you'll actually be spending your waking hours. The purpose of your work can make a big difference in your happiness; to some people, it matters immensely. But if the demands of your job bring out the worst in you, a good mission won't be much consolation. Even if you think your job is a high calling, it's easy to be miserable if you don't like what you're doing all day.

What makes the most difference to your happiness, I suspect, is how it feels to wear the hat. If you don't like reading a lot, don't become an appellate litigator, because appellate litigators read all day. If you don't like tough negotiations, don't become a small-claims lawyer. Your life will be defined just as much by what you do all day as it is by why you do it.

GLADIATORS AND BEYOND

Many people's ideas about what lawyers do begin with the archetype of the litigator—the lawyer who makes arguments to a court, advocating the position of one of the parties to a lawsuit or some other court proceeding. Lawyers who litigate, though, are just one kind of lawyer. In fact, on any given day, most American lawyers are not litigating. Lawyers also act as negotiators, auditors, investigators, teachers, and—especially—counselors.

Every lawyer who has a client has to give advice. Counseling—giving advice—is just as fundamental a lawyerly role as advocacy. Counseling and advocacy are very different modes of lawyering. An advocate's job, most people believe, is to see things from the client's perspective—to be, in effect, biased in favor of whatever arguments will help your client. When you're acting as a counselor, it's extremely important *not* to let your views be biased.

You can choose a career where you won't litigate, but it's almost impossible to avoid counseling. Litigators counsel (they have to advise the client about how the trial is going so that the client can make decisions during the trial), but counselors don't always litigate. There is a long list of legal jobs that don't involve litigation: you can become a transactional lawyer, or work for a corporation's internal legal office, or facilitate negotiations, or run for political office, or work in a policy job in government.

I emphasize this because first-year law students sometimes get the impression that litigation is the heart of what lawyers do—that lawyers are, first and foremost, litigators. It's not unusual to hear a mentor say, "You need some litigation experience." There's an implication, sometimes, that you're not a real lawyer until you've litigated. You rarely hear anyone say, "You need some experience counseling people through difficult decisions," with the implication that *that* will make you a real lawyer. But counseling is a more universal part of the lawyering experience than litigation.

If you say, "She's a good lawyer, but a bad litigator," it's provocative, but intelligible. But if you say, "He's a good lawyer, but he gives terrible legal advice," you're just not making sense. The point is don't be fooled into thinking that the only role available to you is the role of litigator, or that you're not a "real lawyer" unless you litigate. There are lots of kinds of lawyers. And every one of them is real.

WHAT YOU THINK ABOUT

Along with thinking about what kind of *work* fits you best, consider what kind of *thinking* fits you best. For one thing, there's the question of what you'll be thinking about. Imagine any passion, from medieval literature to espionage to shrimp farming: somewhere a lawyer has built a career around that thing. There is almost no sphere of human activity that doesn't interact with the law.

Judge Gerard Lynch tells his mentees that the real divide in the legal profession isn't between public interest and private practice; it's between lawyers who spend most of their time thinking about *facts* and lawyers who spend most of their time thinking about *ideas*. Lawyers who lobby Congress, for example, spend most of their day thinking about legal ideas, regardless of whether they're on the side of big corporations or impoverished children. And lawyers who represent landlords and tenants spend most of their time thinking about the facts of specific relationships, whether they work for David or Goliath. Fact lawyer and idea lawyer are different roles, different kinds of lives.

Again, be skeptical of the subtle messages you might get from law school. Your professors send a powerful message by choosing to emphasize certain skills over others. If first-year classes focus exclusively on the ability to argue about doctrinal questions, they send a certain message about the lawyer's role: *A lawyer's role is to be good at arguing about legal doctrine.* Of course, almost every lawyer needs to be good at arguing about doctrine. But for many lawyers, other skills are just as important: telling stories about facts, negotiating, writing, strategic planning, marketing, political maneuvering, and on and on. Some lawyers hardly argue about doctrine at all. If you're a family-court lawyer, for example, or an immigration lawyer who specializes in asylum cases, the vast bulk of your time may be spent making arguments about a given client's story, rather than the meaning of a legal proposition. Facts, not doctrine, will be the substance of your work. Again, it's hard to know in advance which kind of lawyering role appeals to you more, and it's important to keep an open mind.

I've tried to give you a few different ways to slice the legal world, but there are lots more. Think about which ways of slicing it seem most relevant to you. The goal here is to identify the rewards that each role offers. What kind of satisfactions are you looking for?

Where to Learn about Roles

This chapter's advice has been to think about the career you might pursue in terms of which of the many lawyering roles appeal to you. But that requires getting a sense of what lawyering roles are out there, and that may not be easy. I don't know of any books that map out the different kinds of roles—in fact, I'm not sure a book like that would be possible. We can make generalizations about prosecutors, corporate lawyers, lawyers who practice in small-claims court, and so on, but the day-to-day experiences of lawyers in any of these categories may vary enormously from state to state, city to city, and firm to firm. Different cities have different cultures; the same firm may have an office in New York City where lawyers are expected to work past midnight and a satellite office in a smaller city where the expectations are more humane. Two lawyers may practice the same kind of law, but if one works for a firm that's prestigious and flourishing, and the other works for a firm that struggles to get by, their lives will be very different. And of course the choices that are open to you will depend on the particular law school you graduate from; some schools seem to feed graduates directly to high-prestige clerkships and high-paying Wall Street firms, while many other schools send most of their graduates to small local firms. And of course many law school graduates struggle to find any legal work at all.

So where can you go to learn more about the lawyering roles that are available to you? The best place to start is the career services office of your law school, which should be able to help you get an idea of what networks the law school is tied into, and where graduates tend to go. Use their resources to find graduates who can help you understand what your options are. One perfectly normal practice is to ask alumni for an "informational interview"—meaning a brief session where you sit down and ask them questions about what jobs are out there, what life is like for lawyers in those jobs, and what it takes to get hired for them. If you have a particular passion—shrimp farming, video games, Montana politics, whatever—try to find alumni who share that passion, and ask them how to build a career around it.

It's important to get a sense of what roles are out there, but that's only part of the challenge. It's just as important to look for experience acting in a role, and reflecting on that experience. Many lawyering roles involve acting in ways that are probably new to you: standing up in court to address a judge; giving advice to the senior officers of corporations; helping a mother fight for custody of her children. Until you've experienced something that resembles these kinds of work, it's hard to know whether they're right for you.

So where you can explore the roles you'll be choosing from? Traditional classes may offer you some opportunity to learn about lawyers' roles, but if your classes follow the traditional Socratic pattern—in which the professor asks students to defend arguments for and against the conclusions of the judges whose opinions they read—you're really exploring just one kind of lawyering role, the role of advocate. Traditional classes may implicitly exaggerate the importance of this kind of role. While there's no doubt that many lawyers make arguments about propositions of law, many other lawyers' work centers around the giving of advice, rather than the presentation of argument. So remember that the role you're asked to play in class is not necessarily the role that you'll play as a lawyer.

Nontraditional classes may give you a chance to explore other kinds of roles. Clinics, in particular, offer you the opportunity for experience and informed reflection about the role you play. They let you test your ideas about lawyering and lawyering roles against real-world challenges and experiences. Of course, you may not be able to experience exactly the kind of work you hope to make a career out of—there are few law school clinics in which you give advice to a corporation debating the merits of a mega-merger, for example. But you can get experience, in clinics and other nontraditional classes, playing the role of an advocate, or a counselor, or a negotiator, and each of these experiences—combined with the reflection that your professors and colleagues can help guide you through—will help you understand much better what it means to play each of these roles.

Externships are also worth mentioning. They give you the opportunity to work in a law office off campus, observing (and helping) real lawyers at work. The question to ask about any externship is whether it will include opportunities for reflection on what you're learning.

There are other nontraditional classes that might give you some opportunity to reflect on the process of getting into character. Many law schools offer classes that let you play the role of a lawyer arguing in court, negotiating, counseling a client, preparing a witness, or investigating facts. These skills classes involve learning to do the specific tasks that lawyers perform. Ideally, simulation classes like these provide an opportunity for reflection on the lawyer's role—if a lawyer needs to be able to deliver a compelling oral argument, then what kinds of qualities should she try to develop in herself? If a lawyer needs to be a negotiator, then what are the ways of understanding her role that will best prepare her to negotiate well?

Of the simulation classes, classes on negotiation and alternative dispute resolution (ADR) may be the most likely to involve serious examination of lawyering roles. The field of ADR has, in the last thirty years or so, produced serious theoretical challenges to traditional ideas about lawyering and lawyering roles. ADR theorists have questioned the whole idea of litigation as an approach to conflict resolution. As a result, studying ADR theory is a great way to expose some of the basic assumptions we often make about the qualities that make lawyers effective. Toughness might be a virtue in adversarial litigation, for example, but in other contexts, other qualities might be more useful; one ADR expert's list of more desirable qualities includes "creativity, patience, persistence, flexibility, and resilience."[7] Learning to think about what qualities a given role requires can have benefits far beyond the context of negotiations; it will help you think critically and creatively about your role as a lawyer when you eventually start working as one.

Extracurricular activities can give you other opportunities to explore your role. A tax law club, for example, might give you a chance to learn more about what tax lawyers do. (If you're wondering whether I'm going to make a joke about tax lawyers, I'm not. Tax law can be fascinating.) Other clubs might give you experience simulating a role. A mock trial society, for example, will give you experience acting as a trial lawyer—which, admittedly, is not as useful an experience as doing real trial work, but it's much more informative than watching trial lawyers on TV.

Remember that the goal isn't just to try on the lawyering roles that interest you, but to understand them better. Understanding what it means to play the role of a trial lawyer is useful for any lawyer, even one who never sets foot in a courtroom, because all lawyers occasionally have to interact with trial lawyers, and if you don't understand the work they do, you may find them a pretty confusing species. And as you start to approach your own career choices, you'll want to know more than just which kinds of lawyerly activities seem fun; you'll want to know which roles you'll find meaningful. Reflection on the various lawyering roles tends to lead to reflection on your own values and life goals—your professional identity, which the next chapter discusses.

The problem is not that students do not know whether they want to be lawyers. They are not sure what kind of *people* they want to be.

DUNCAN KENNEDY

16 The Person under the Hat

You will be transformed by law school. By the time it's over, you'll talk a bit differently and think a bit differently. Things that once felt strange will begin to feel natural: speaking in public, or wearing a suit, or taking both sides in an argument. You might come to value different things. As you learn to inhabit a new professional role, you'll develop a new professional identity.

The changes will probably be subtle—you won't go from Jekyll to Hyde, or vice versa—but they'll be real. To some extent, they'll be beyond your control. Law school is a pressure cooker, and nobody emerges wholly unchanged. But you're not just a noodle waiting for law school to boil you. The professional identity you develop is formed in large part by the choices you make. This chapter will talk about those choices: why it's worth thinking about your professional identity, what threatens to disrupt that process and leave you confused and unhappy, and how to anchor yourself against those threats.

Let me be a little more clear about my terms. The last chapter talked about your *professional role*, which I defined as the expectations that people have about how you will behave in the context of your work as a lawyer. Your role isn't just something that's imposed on you; you have some power to influence people's expectations. You always have the option of negotiating, of trying to change their minds about what they should expect from you. When you do negotiate your role, and when you make decisions about whether a given role is right for you, what drives you is your beliefs about lawyering and the things you value. Those beliefs and values are the core of your professional identity—the person you are, or the person you aspire to be, under your professional hat. That's what this chapter is about.

A big part of your professional identity is your goals and preferences: What do you get out of lawyering? What professional experiences make you feel satisfied and rewarded? What in your legal work contributes to your professional and personal well-being? In other words, what drives you? You'll feel that some cases are important and others aren't. Why? What makes a case matter to you—is it that some important public policy is implicated, or that a lot of money is at risk, or that your client really cares about the case? What kinds of cases do you hope to work on, and what kinds of cases do you hope to avoid? Your answers form a set of attitudes about the work you do, and these attitudes are part of your professional identity.

Your identity is also made up of your ethics and your values. As a law student, I hoped that my professional responsibility class would help answer questions about what I, as a lawyer, should value. It didn't. Instead we studied rules of conduct, interspersed with a series of painful dilemmas that seemed to have no answer. I wanted answers! Or at least a method. As I've learned since, there *are* ethical theories and methods out there that can help prod and clarify your thinking about tough ethical questions.[1] But when you face a real dilemma, a genuine conflict of values, a theory alone won't get you the answer. General principles can help, but your understanding of who you are and what you value has to take you the rest of the way.

Your professional identity is also a matter of style. For example, there's your way of speaking: Do you go for grand flights of rhetoric, or simple speech in plain English? Passion or understatement?

Your style also involves the mood in which you approach your work. Consider this sentence about the rituals and the experience of lawyering, from an article by Linda Meyer:

> Perhaps the smell of leather and mold, the opposition of counsel tables, the elevation of the jury, the black robes, the etiquette and ritual, gather the quietness, the solemnity, the sense of history, heaviness, consequence, and blood, that is necessary for stern and thoughtful work.[2]

Is that how lawyering feels to you? Consider, as an alternative, the lawyer in Hunter S. Thompson's *Fear and Loathing in Las Vegas*, who is introduced to us with this sentence: "My attorney had taken his shirt off and was pouring beer on his chest, to facilitate the tanning process." There are many styles. Your identity is a matter of how lawyering feels to you, the *moods* of practice. Are you a stern-and-thoughtful-work lawyer, or a pouring-beer-on-yourself lawyer? There are, it seems, many alternatives.

The best reason to spend time and energy thinking about your professional identity may be the fact that a lot of lawyers are unhappy. Depression and alcoholism afflict us at twice the rate of the general population. (Law students start off with the same rates as everyone else.) Depression rates skyrocket during the first year of law school, and never return to normal.[3] This suggests that a lot of lawyers are getting it wrong. They pick a job, but they pick the wrong one. They think they know what's valuable in a lawyer's life, but they find out too late that they had the wrong idea. Their ideas lead them to places they wish they hadn't gone.

Of course, I can't prove that there's any connection between lawyers' unhappiness and failure to think skeptically about lawyerly roles and identities. For all I know, the happiest lawyers might be the ones who accept their role thoughtlessly. But I doubt that willfully ignoring questions like these ever helps anyone achieve well-being. If you're entering a profession with high levels of unhappiness, anxiety, and psychological disorder—a profession that lots of people are struggling mightily to leave—you might do well to pay attention to what kind of life you're putting together for yourself.

It's not just lawyers who feel trapped in their roles—law school itself can be painful if the role you're getting into isn't the right one for you. Some law students feel profoundly alienated by law school. They say that they feel as if law school was forcing them to become someone they didn't want to be. They feel as if their values are threatened, as if their personality is being changed in ways they don't like. Of course, it's good to have your values challenged. Questioning students' deepest values was Socrates's method. But law school shouldn't make you loathe yourself.

A series of studies have concluded that the students who feel most alienated by law school are disproportionately women.[4] The average woman in law school speaks less often and has a worse experience than the average man.[5] Some research suggests that women—more often than men—tend to *lose* confidence in their professional abilities during law school. In one study, 51 percent of women law students said that although they felt intelligent and articulate prior to law school, they did not feel that way now. Only 29 percent of men felt the same.[6] Other studies have shown that women emerge from law school less confident than men, even when they perform just as well.[7] One book on women's experience in law school, pointedly titled *Becoming Gentlemen*, argues that the role law school presses on students is a gender role as well as a professional role.[8] (Think of the metaphors used to describe lawyers: hired gun, pit bull, gladiator. When you hear those phrases, do you picture a woman?) Others disagree.

There's also disagreement about why women might find law school alienating. Maybe women learn differently from men, and the Socratic method naturally favors the way men learn. Or maybe the fault lies less with the method and more with bad professors who create macho atmospheres in which women are silenced. Are students alienated when the Socratic method is done wrong, or when it's done right?

Race, too, seems to have an effect. Students of color participate in class less often than white students.[9] A recent study found that there was no disparity in sense of belonging between white and nonwhite students as they entered law school—but by the end of the first semester, students of color had begun to feel more alienated, more isolated, and less confident in their academic abilities.[10]

Whatever the reason for these disparities, students of all races and genders sometimes find the experience coercive and corrupting, and want to resist the transformation it seems to demand. All law students may feel constrained, challenged, threatened, and baffled by their new roles. It's easy to find criticisms of law school's effects on students' identities; one essay by a Harvard Law student compares law school to "total institutions" like prisons or psychiatric hospitals, and argues that it effectively erases its students' identities in favor of a bland, helpless, and pathetic new sense of self.[11]

If you're wondering what kind of life awaits you in the legal profession, it's perhaps an ominous sign that the literary works most often referenced in judicial opinions are Orwell's *1984* and Kafka's *The Trial*.[12] But things don't have to be grim. Lawyering can be deeply satisfying. It can be fun. There are lots of happy lawyers, and, contrary to what you might have heard, there are happy law students too. The trick is to find what's good in the new roles you're exploring. I don't mean what's good in an abstract, objective sense; I mean what's good *for you*. It will be a struggle, and there will be many ways to lose your path.

Whoever you are, and whatever your reasons for questioning the role you're taking on, skepticism about the identity law school presses on you is a good idea. You don't have to accept the version of the lawyerly role that others offer. There's no right way to be a lawyer.

The Storms That Blow You Off Course

It's easy to find stories about lawyers whose lives have gone wrong. Sometimes the crash is spectacular: a corporate meltdown in which we discover that a well-respected lawyer was helping corporate officers defraud their shareholders, or a report that a bank's lawyers tried to collect $500,000 on a mortgage when they knew perfectly well that the homeowner only owed half that much.[13] The more disturbing stories, to me, are the ones that don't make headlines: the stories about lawyers who are quietly miserable, who've lost respect for themselves, who get nothing out of their jobs but don't know what to do about it. Or the lawyers who say things about their work that make you wonder whether they have any respect for themselves, like the Wall Street lawyer who told a startled audience, "We *pride* ourselves on being assholes. It's part of the firm culture."[14]

The question I want to talk about is why lawyers' identities sometimes go wrong, and what can be done about it. My theory is that most lawyers (or, at least, most of the people who've read this far in a chapter about professional identity) don't start out wanting to be sleazy or evil. American lawyers are favorably regarded by just 25 percent of the American public, which makes us one of the least popular American professions.[15] Few lawyers launch their careers thinking, "Let's see if I can help cut it down to 20 percent." And nobody starts their career wanting to be miserable.

Why do some lawyers sometimes turn into such awful people? Why do lawyers sometimes stay in jobs they loathe? One answer is that they were evil or weak willed to begin with, and of course some of them probably were. But I don't think that's the whole story.

Think about what happens when we face a choice that implicates our values—by which I mean both our beliefs about what's right and wrong and our beliefs about what really matters. It's natural to assume certain things about what happens in situations where our values are implicated. We assume that conflicts will help us learn about our values. If we do things that conflict with our values, we'll feel torn and conflicted. Those bad feelings will protect us, we assume, against doing the wrong thing in the future—if we do something that conflicts with who we really are, it will hurt, and we'll remember that it hurt, and we won't do it again.

In fact, what happens is sometimes just the opposite: our values change to fit our experiences. In our minds, what we've done *becomes* right and good, just because it's what we've done. Consider this study: The psychologist Judson Mills gave middle school students a test on which it seemed relatively easy to cheat. (In fact, Mills was watching them.) He offered gift certificates to the best performers. Some students cheated, while others didn't. Before and after the test, Mills measured their attitudes toward cheating, to see if they changed. The students who cheated later became more lenient toward cheating. The students who resisted the temptation also changed their views of cheating—they condemned it more strongly than they had before.[16] When Mills varied the incentive—offering even more of a reward for high scores—he found that he produced even more of a change in the views of students who resisted the temptation. Their newly severe views on cheating seemed to come from their experience resisting it.[17]

The mechanism here is called *cognitive dissonance*.[18] The students who resisted the temptation to cheat had conflicting thoughts: On the one hand, they thought, *I really wanted that gift certificate. I could easily have gotten it by cheating.* On the other hand, they also thought, *I chose not to cheat.* The best way to ease the dissonance of that thought, Mills concluded, was for the students to decide *I must strongly disapprove of cheating.* Which is why the students condemned cheating even more strongly when the temptation they had resisted was bigger: the bigger the temptation, the bigger the dissonance of having resisted it. The students who did cheat, not surprisingly, strengthened their belief that cheating wasn't all that bad.[19]

Think of these experiments as you consider how a certain job or role might affect your identity. If you become a criminal defense lawyer, your role may require you to suggest to juries that the criminal justice system is unfair. If you become a prosecutor, your role may require you to assert with deep feeling that it isn't. Dissonance theory says that you're likely to come to believe the positions you advocate. Your role's influences are subtle, but they can cause profound changes.

Dissonance theory has important implications for how you reflect on your role and your identity. Over time, your professional identity—your understanding of yourself, your values, your goals, and your style—may come to line up surprisingly well with the role you play. Because once you've begun playing a role, it may be hard to keep your role (what other people expect from you) separate from your identity (how you see yourself). *I do this for a living* and *this isn't who I am* are powerfully dissonant thoughts. So when you reflect on your professional identity—when you think about whether you're becoming the person you want to become—it's not enough just to look at the choices you've made and ask yourself how you feel about them. Your brain will be struggling hard to find reasons to say, "I feel OK." You need to find ways to challenge yourself—to get past the dissonance— but, unfortunately, psychologists haven't found any cure for dissonance, or even an easy way around it. When popular books by psychologists talk about cognitive dissonance, the only constructive advice they seem to offer is, essentially, to be aware of the phenomenon and be reflective about your decisions.[20] The best defense is to get into the habit of asking yourself tough questions about what you really want. This may work better if you reflect on these questions out loud, with friends, because your friends have an easier time seeing your situation clearly. *My friend is playing the wrong role* is a less painful thought than *I'm playing the wrong role.* So maybe your friends will be less vulnerable to the kind of dissonance that might cloud your judgment.

Along with reflection, you'll also need to build a resilient framework of your own values and aspirations, so that when they're challenged, your framework can resist. The next section will suggest some ways that can work.

Virtues and Other Anchors

I spoke earlier about the rewards offered by different kinds of lawyering roles. The rewards can include prestige, power, money, the pursuit of social justice, human connection, the pleasure of serving people in need, accomplishment in craft, and more. Some of these rewards are external benefits, like prestige and money. Some of the rewards are an intrinsic part of law practice, like accomplishment in the craft. Some, like justice, are both. No job or role offers you all of the possible rewards. You'll have to choose which rewards to pursue.

Each of the various kinds of rewards requires certain qualities in the lawyer who hopes to achieve them. For example, you can't enjoy the pleasures of serving people unless you have some degree of empathy and kindness. You can't accomplish the rewards of commercial success (wealth, power, etc.) unless you have some measure of business sense. You can't become accomplished in the craft of law unless you're patient, diligent, thorough, and so on.

So each reward implies a set of lawyerly virtues. There is an endless list of qualities a lawyer might aspire to cultivate: dignity, aggressiveness, loyalty, caring, ambition, respect, and on and on. Each of these qualities can become a vice if pushed far enough. It's possible to be loyal to a fault, or independent to a fault; it's possible to be aggressive to a fault, or accommodating to a fault; it's possible to be too clever, too forthcoming, or too compassionate, depending on the situation. Every choice is about finding the right balance, the right quality for the situations you encounter.

I suggest thinking about your professional identity in terms of the qualities you aspire to cultivate in yourself. The way you identify those qualities is by thinking about what good things you want to find in law practice. But *what do I want to achieve?* is only the first question. The real question is *what must I become to achieve those things?*

One example of a lawyerly virtue is explored at length in Anthony Kronman's book *The Lost Lawyer,* which focuses on practical wisdom. Practical wisdom, as Kronman sees it, is a kind of good judgment, but it's a very specific kind of good judgment; it involves a particular disposition, a way of looking at the world. A lawyer, Kronman says, must be both compassionate and detached: compassionate, because the lawyer has to be able to understand the client's situation to help the client make choices, and detached because a decision must be made, and the lawyer's role is to help the client step back from the press of the situation and see things clearly.[21] Kronman points out that these qualities, the sympathy and detachment that make up practical wisdom, aren't just lawyerly virtues; they're human virtues. Which is why, for Kronman, law is worth pursuing: it requires the cultivation of qualities that make you a better person. But he takes a fairly gloomy view of the legal profession, because he thinks too many law jobs don't allow the cultivation of practical wisdom.

Kronman's view of what qualities a lawyer should cultivate is just one view. There are a wide range of ideas within the profession about what makes a lawyer good and what's good about being a lawyer. Some lawyers would say that good lawyering is primarily an intellectual accomplishment, and that the virtues of a lawyer are mainly intellectual ones. For others, law is a business, and the lawyerly virtues are the same as the virtues of any other businessperson: industriousness, creativity, inventiveness, social skill, and so on. Still other lawyers think that lawyers' main function is to bring about justice, and so the virtues lawyers need are things like courage, determination, and a functioning moral compass. And others might say that lawyers are problem solvers, or something else entirely. There are lots of possible views, each of which entails a set of ideas about what virtues a lawyer needs.

It would be nice to give you a list of the virtues different kinds of lawyers need. But there are just too many different views; there isn't even a well-developed controversy I can summarize for you. You'll have to put together your own sense of what virtues are worth struggling toward.

What's clear is that there is no one answer to the question of what qualities a lawyer needs. Every lawyer needs a complicated balance of virtues, not just one. A lawyer who thinks law is purely a business, for example, and that a business's only social responsibility is value creation, still needs a sense of right and wrong. You can't represent clients well in court unless you can anticipate the judge's reaction to your arguments. Unless you have a functioning moral compass of your own, you won't be able to predict which way someone else's moral compass will point. You can never pick just one virtue and devote yourself to it; there's always a trade-off.

Thinking about your professional identity in terms of the rewards you're after, and the virtues it will take to achieve them, may help you build a framework for thinking about your identity that's less vulnerable to pressures like cognitive dissonance. If you reflect well on who you want to become, you'll be better able to resist those pressures when they start pushing you in the wrong direction.

It's important to get into the habit of reflecting on your professional identity now, in law school, before you start your practice. Understand why you committed to law school—what you hoped the rewards would be, and who you hoped you would become—so that later, when you've developed new goals and aspirations, you can compare them and gauge whether you're heading in a healthy direction. One of the best ways to reflect on your professional identity is to reflect on how it's changed, and why.

There are some useful things you can do now, as a law student, to protect yourself from the kinds of slippery slopes that lead to problems with your professional identity later. One thing you can do is to reflect not just on your goals and values, but on specific commitments you can make now, in law school, to stop yourself from sliding down slippery slopes later. David Luban suggests that lawyers who are concerned about the ethical effects of the job they're entering should set bright lines for themselves before they get into the job. If you're becoming a prosecutor, for example, and you're concerned about protecting your integrity, you might promise yourself that you'll never prosecute a defendant you believe to be innocent. Luban writes:

> The formula is simple: "Whatever else I do, and however else my views change, I will never, ever . . ." You name it. Cover up someone else's crime. Lie about money. Falsify a document. Let a colleague suffer the consequences for my own screw-up. Do something where I couldn't look my father in the eye if I told him about it.[22]

Commitments like these can serve as anchors when situations become turbulent. When you find yourself pressed by the situation, or when everyone around you seems to agree on something that feels wrong to you, commitments like these can give you a reference outside the situation, something to grab hold of.

You have to be careful not to choose these anchors too quickly. The ethical complexities of a given job are usually not clear until you've worked in it for a while. You will change your beliefs and values as you go through your working life; you *should* change them. (Would a career be worth having if it didn't change a single belief about things that matter?) So be aware that change can be a good thing, and don't choose these anchors lightly; make sure they're things that really matter.

Dropping anchor in the way Luban suggests isn't just a good idea for protecting yourself from ethical corruption; it can be a powerful way of protecting other aspects of your professional identity. Promise that the day you find yourself pretending to agree with your boss because you don't feel comfortable expressing disagreement, you'll start looking for another job. Or the day you realize your job isn't mentally challenging. Or the day you realize you're not helping anyone.

Reflecting on the qualities you want to cultivate in yourself is the flip side of Luban's the-day-I-quit-my-job strategy. Don't just think about what you dread; think about what you hope for. *I want to become a craftsperson,* you might think. If excellence in craft is the professional virtue you most want to cultivate, it makes sense to anchor yourself in terms of that goal: *The day I realize I'm just a technician, I'll move on.*

Those two ideas—the qualities you aspire to cultivate, and the promises you make about things you'll never accept—go together. Each of them is a distillation of a long process of reflection on what matters to you, a clear way of expressing—in a way that will stay with you into the future, into situations where your identity comes under pressure—why you wanted to go into law in the first place, and what you hope to find there.

Justice Cardozo said to her, as she began practice, " . . . You will be a good lawyer because you have infinite curiosity."

THOMAS SHAFFER

Conclusion: The Questions You'll Ask

I want to end the book with one last thought about what makes it possible for a law student to do well. I want to focus on just one of the many qualities a law student might aspire to develop—one that will sometimes need to be balanced against other demands, but one that seems, to me, central to what makes some law students flourish in law school while others struggle.

In each of the areas where law school challenges you, the law student who thrives is often the law student who is able to be enthusiastically skeptical: questioning the advice that others offer, asking of any approach, "What are the flaws here? What could go wrong?" It wouldn't make sense to say, "She's a great law student, but she always asks the wrong question."

The ability to ask good questions is more than a skill. It's a habit, a learned disposition. It's what reflection is really about. Healthy skepticism isn't just a tendency to interrogate people, or a reluctance to believe things. It's the ability to ask a question that gets right to the fundamental weakness in an argument, or a question that reframes the issue in a more useful way, or a question that provokes a new way of thinking about a problem.

The word "reflection" often implies something slow. It needn't. The skeptical law student hears an argument and immediately asks what arguments could be made on the other side; that's what classes train you to do. The skeptical law student approaches decisions about careers, roles, and ethics, with the same inquisitive excitement. It's *energetic* reflection that I'm recommending, not cynicism, rumination, or navel-gazing. Good questions accompanied by a smile tend to be called "curiosity," and good questions accompanied by a frown tend to be called "skepticism." You want both: skepticism and curiosity, blended together.

A good law student never takes "just because" for an answer. Neither does a good lawyer. Great lawyers are skeptical—in the sense of taking nothing for granted—without being cynical. I'm not urging you to be a reflexive curmudgeon who attacks every idea. The skeptical curiosity I'm talking about is a hopeful, engaged kind of attentiveness. The best law students launch themselves into each new question, asking, "What does this class offer? Where are the new ideas?" Real curiosity requires hope and optimism.

Cynicism isn't useful, because just criticizing other people's ideas won't get you very far. You need to generate alternative ideas to get anywhere. And you have to be willing to generate dumb ones. Television writers sometimes pass a "stupid stick" around the writers' room; whoever holds the stupid stick is free to offer any idea with a guarantee that nobody will think less of them if it's stupid.[1] The most effective law students carry a stupid stick with them everywhere.

Part of the disposition I'm describing is having an open mind. On the first day of law school, you will carry a lot of expectations about what classes will be like, what law will be like, what you are supposed to be learning. Your classes may not meet these expectations. It would be surprising if they did. The law students who thrive will be the law students who adapt to the changes, who embrace the new questions they're learning to ask.

You may find yourself wondering, *Why did the professor assign us law review articles about libertarianism instead of teaching us the black-letter law?* It's a reasonable question. Some people will shrug and say to themselves, *Because this is all a bunch of crap.* That group will not do well. Others will say, *Here I am in a state of uncertainty,* and stay there for a while to see what can be made of it. When the professor's not making sense, they don't panic. They sit with it for a while, trying to put their finger on just what it is they don't understand. They accept that uncertainty is a normal part of learning.

Reflection is often what carries you through the difficult parts of law school. A sensible law student looks at exams and asks, *How should I shape my semester's work in light of the exam's structure?* You have to reflect constantly on your work over the semester, asking whether it's helping you move toward the ultimate goal. When I talk about asking good questions, I mean the whole process of staying skeptical about what works and what doesn't, and staying curious about what ideas you might have missed.

Each of the skills involved in "thinking like a lawyer" is bound up with the ability to ask the right questions. Issue spotting, of course, *is* the skill of asking good questions. Legal argument might be described as the ability to probe deeply into the best possible ideas on either side of a debate. The skill of legal argument depends on taking nothing for granted.

And distilling, too, has a lot to do with questions. Distilling is about looking at what you read and asking, *What's this really about? What's the core idea here?* Psychologists have studied the effects of asking questions on learning; they've found that when you ask yourself questions about what you read, you remember it better.[2]

The study methods I've described in this book all revolve around the central idea of reflecting on what you've read. Taking notes and outlining, as I've described them, are ways of asking yourself questions about the law you're studying. *What did that case say? What did the professor mean?* The habit of asking yourself questions like these is one of the most important skills a law student can develop.

When you begin practicing law, too, asking questions will be a core skill. Good practical judgment requires reflection. Reflection is the process of asking yourself questions: *what went well in that negotiation; what didn't?* Reflection can be taught and learned and talked about. It's something you practice and get better at over the years. Ideally, it's something you do with other people, so that their ideas can inform your own.

The ability to ask the right question might be most important of all when it comes to choosing between jobs. You'll have to think carefully about which jobs are the good jobs, to listen skeptically to other people's advice. It's important not to be driven by everyone else's sense of what's prestigious and what's not, or who's a real lawyer and who isn't. The habit of asking good questions can protect you from stumbling into the wrong role.

Just as important is keeping an open mind and staying curious. I have a friend who had long aspired to be a criminal defense lawyer. At a law school career fair, he submitted his resume to a bunch of organizations, and—by mistake—included a prosecutor's office on a list. (That particular office was ambiguously named.) He didn't realize his mistake until he walked into the interview, and the interviewer asked him, "Why do you want to be a prosecutor?" He made something up. But by the end of the interview, he was intrigued. He went back for a second interview. When I met him twenty years later, he was one of the happiest prosecutors in the business.

Similarly, there's an appellate attorney I know of who has a very quiet voice. This is generally seen as a handicap in a professional public speaker. But she's turned it to her advantage. She never tries to speak loudly or powerfully. She just stands at the podium and waits for total silence before she begins. The effect is dramatic, and—because she usually has something to say that was worth waiting for—it works well. Keep an open mind about yourself, your skills, what roles you're suited for. Don't assume you're not suited for a job just because you seem different from some of the people who are good at it. The thing that you think disqualifies you might turn out, on reflection, to be a gift.

Reflection is also critical to maintaining your integrity as a lawyer. Discussing the ethical traps that many lawyers fall into, David Luban suggests "chronic skepticism and discomfort with oneself."[3] As we saw in part 4, there are powerful situational and social influences that can move you slowly and gently down the road to becoming a person you don't want to be. And it's not just ourselves we need to question. We need to question our work, our ideas, and our colleagues too. You practice the skill of asking questions so that it's there when you need it.

You can't ask good questions unless you learn to be comfortable in a state of uncertainty. That uncertain feeling—the feeling of not knowing what's going on—is what learning feels like. It's a necessary part of learning new areas of law, and of understanding the stories and values of a new client, and of figuring out what's important in any unfamiliar situation. So getting used to that dizzy sense of uncertainty is good practice for lawyering. You'll spend much of your first year in law school feeling deeply uncertain. That's how it's supposed to feel.

It's not just learning to be uncertain; it's learning to be wrong. Carla Needleman, writing about pottery, says that one of the defining virtues of a good craftsperson is the ability to fail. "I insisted on my right to consider [my] plates failures, not successes, because I wanted to go on."[4] Each project is successful in some ways and unsuccessful in others, and if you don't see how each project failed, you don't learn anything you can bring with you to the next project. What would you do differently if you could do it again? There's always something. Lawyers leaving courtrooms always think of one great thing they could have said but didn't. It feels painful when the snappy retort pops into your head on the way out. But it's a good thing when this happens. It means the brain is still working when the argument is over. It's what learning from experience feels like. If you stifle that urge—if you say to yourself, *That was good enough*, before you've thought about how the work could have come out differently—you're not asking the right questions.

All of this may help to explain why the first year of law school has to hurt so much. Good teachers have to be unsettling: they have to help the students develop the habit of asking fundamental, uncomfortable questions. Needleman writes that teachers must "arouse in the student the emotional need to approach the craft differently by blocking in him any satisfaction that can be found in his customary means of approach."[5] Teachers have to help you learn to feel uncertain and unsatisfied, because that's where questions come from.

But that's not all teachers have to help you do. Law professors sometimes miss this next point, which Needleman puts well: When someone is always saying "No" to you—as law professors always are—it can be hard to learn anything "unless the 'No' is grounded in a bigger 'Yes.'"[6] If there's no sense of hope and joyful curiosity behind the interrogations students suffer in the first-year classroom, they may be driven into cynicism, rejecting everything, or into passivity, questioning nothing. There's a difference between the kind of question that drives on toward deeper understanding and the kind of question that convinces you you're small.

Some of your professors will understand this and some won't. But the questions they ask you aren't nearly as important as the questions you ask yourself. That's what I mean when I say your reflection should be energetic: always ground your "No" in a bigger "Yes."

Before Elena Kagan was a Supreme Court justice, she wrote an article about what made a judge of her acquaintance great. She said he was

> a prober. He is constantly asking why the problems before him have arisen—what features of the world are responsible for the parties' conflicts and their inability to resolve them. He is always exploring why legal doctrines are the way they are—behind the boilerplate statements and string citations provided by the litigants, what purposes and goals the law is seeking to serve.[7]

The same could be said of many great lawyers, maybe all great lawyers. Being a prober, in law, is one of the most useful things you can aspire to. Lawyers need to understand the real facts of a situation before they try to manipulate it. They need to understand why rules exist before they try to invoke them. Lawyers deal with ideas, and with people, and there's a great deal to be learned about both—more than could ever be taught in a three-year curriculum, no matter how well structured.

Being a prober can be endlessly rewarding. For the curious lawyer, there's an infinite repository of useful things to learn about, in the real world and in books. We sometimes have a habit of using the words "intellectual" and "practical" as if they were opposed to each other. But the world of law practice shows what a mistake that is. A lawyer's job is to answer questions like *What will persuade that judge?* and *What would be the best rule to apply in this case?* These are questions that psychologists and economists and legal theorists have been studying for years. Nobody could ever master all these fields. But it's hard to see how any lawyer can ignore them. That's why I've tried, throughout this book, to mention some of the more interesting writers and researchers I've come across, both in the world of legal theory and in the social sciences that overlap with it. I wanted to give you a sense of how thrilled I've been as a young lawyer to discover some of the fascinating fields of inquiry that overlap with law. I wanted to give you a sense of how *useful* they can be.

And that's just the books. Jurisprudence, economics, and psychology are great things for a lawyer to learn about, but of course the real learning happens off the bookshelf, when you apply those ideas to your practice and your life, and when your experience gives you ideas of your own. The choices you make in your practice are your education; the people you meet are your education; the situations that challenge you are your education. These are the rewards of our practice.

Becoming a good lawyer means taking your education seriously long after law school ends. A lawyer's work is made up of words, ideas, and human relationships. It's our business to understand how people think, what matters to them, and why they believe the things they do. The skills and qualities required to learn about these things—being inquisitive, and skeptical, and skilled at reflection—aren't just lawyerly virtues; they're human virtues. We're blessed to be in a profession that calls for knowledge of so many important things.

In our profession, it's possible to be knowledgeable about things that matter. It's possible to become wise, and just, and profoundly useful, if you choose to pursue those goals. Let your inquiring mind be your compass. When you finish law school, *your* education—the one you design and control, the one in which you'll find your place among the many kinds of lawyer it is possible to be—finally begins.

ACKNOWLEDGMENTS

Lots of people have influenced this book, directly and indirectly, from my professors at Georgetown University Law Center and the judges for whom I clerked to the grimly determined preacher whose booming sermons—directed at me and other hapless commuters on the Staten Island Ferry while I tried to bang out a first draft on my laptop—may have given me the idea for the sample exam question about a religion based on belligerence. Other important indirect influences included the professors who wrote the law review articles cited in this book—which, if you read them, will persuade you that when lawyers and judges complain about legal scholarship being dull or irrelevant, it proves only that they're reading the wrong articles.

More direct influences included the people who read drafts and offered thoughtful reactions and suggestions: Rajit Dosanjh, Erin Edmison, David Finkelstein, Chisun Lee, Emily Epstein Leiderman, David Koplow, Michael Miller, Andrea Oser, Julie O'Sullivan, Philip Schrag, and two peer reviewers for the University of Chicago Press. I'm particularly grateful for suggestions and detailed editing by Jenny Gavacs; her contributions improved the book immeasurably. I'm also grateful to several law students who test-drove the book by reading it while they struggled through their first year: Christopher Dunham, Peter Maggiore, Elizabeth Moran, Benjamin Thompson, and Brendan Venter.

Barbara Underwood shaped the book both through her comments on the manuscript and through the thoughtful guidance and mentoring she's given me as a new attorney in the New York State Solicitor General's office. (Her thoughts on the book, I have to note, were provided in a private capacity. All of the views expressed in this book should be attributed only to me, in my private capacity, and not to the Solicitor General's Office.)

My mother, Lauren Ayers, read an early draft with gleeful enthusiasm. As the author of several books herself, she found the idea of a book by her son exciting beyond words. But she passed away before I started looking for a publisher, and it seems profoundly unfair to me that she never got to see it on a bookshelf.

My father, James Ayers, is, thankfully, still around. He read and commented on no less than four successive drafts, and virtually all of the ideas in the book were hashed out during long conversations in which he challenged and scrutinized each one. Those conversations were the best part of the writing process.

Many of the hours that went into the writing of this book were hours when someone was watching my two children, Violet and Evelyn. (Hi Violet! Hi Eve!) I'm especially grateful to my mom and dad, Miriam Trementozzi, Barbara and Thomas Mitchell, Sujathi Mitchell, and Sudha Mitchell.

Beyond everything else, I'm grateful to Emily, more than I could ever say.

SUGGESTIONS FOR
FURTHER READING

Karl Llewellyn's *The Bramble Bush* is worth the attention of every law student; it's funny, idiosyncratic, and passionate. But think carefully before you follow any particular piece of study advice—it was written in 1930, and many things about law school have changed since then.

The best book on issue spotting I know is *Getting to Maybe: How to Excel on Law School Exams*, by Richard Michael Fischl and Jeremy Paul. Its focus, as you'll gather from the title, is exams, and it contains a great deal of excellent advice about exam taking. But it's best read as a book about issue spotting. It gives a detailed taxonomy of the kinds of issues that law students must learn to spot, and quite a lot of sound advice about legal thinking in general.

A dazzlingly good general introduction to legal reasoning is Frederick Schauer's *Thinking Like a Lawyer: A New Introduction to Legal Reasoning*. On legal argument, the book *Making Your Case: The Art of Persuading Judges*, by Antonin Scalia and Bryan Garner, is excellent. You needn't be a fan of Justice Scalia's jurisprudence to appreciate the book.

As for policy arguments, Ward Farnsworth's *The Legal Analyst: A Toolkit For Thinking about the Law* is a great introduction to basic policy arguments about consequences, including arguments about incentives and fun concepts from game theory that sometimes figure in first-year classes. But it doesn't say much about the other kind of policy arguments, arguments about justice. I don't know of any good introductions to arguments about justice that are designed specifically for law students. But Michael Sandel's book *Justice: What's the Right Thing to Do?*, a distillation of his legendarily popular class at Harvard (the class itself is now available on DVD and on the

Internet), is an excellent introduction to philosophical arguments about justice, which might turn out to be handier than you think.

If you're interested in writing a Note, or in doing any serious writing about law, Eugene Volokh's book *Academic Legal Writing* is extremely helpful. It covers all of the questions you're likely to have—how to come up with topic ideas, how to make sure your idea is interesting, how to have a point, how to organize the piece—clearly and well.

On negotiation skills, a great place to start is *Getting to Yes*, by William L. Ury, Roger Fisher, and Bruce M. Patton, researchers of the Harvard Negotiation Project. Although it's written for a popular audience, its explanation of the theory of negotiation has been extremely influential among scholars, and it challenges some widespread intuitions about how to negotiate. It's also a fun read.

On legal writing, start with Bryan Garner's *The Elements of Legal Style*. It's a sort of manifesto for good legal writing, and Garner's writing is itself so good that you carry away a joyful sense of what good writing feels like. That sense of pleasure is what you need most.

If you're concerned with how your professional writing shapes your identity, there is a wonderful book by James Boyd White called *The Legal Imagination*, which presses you to think seriously about how legal writing changes the way you think. It's a hopeful book, and hope is always a good place to start.

ABOUT THE AUTHOR

Andrew Ayers graduated first in his law school class at Georgetown in 2005. He then clerked for the Honorable Sonia Sotomayor on the US Court of Appeals for the Second Circuit, and for the Honorable Gerard E. Lynch on the US District Court for the Southern District of New York. During the second clerkship, he and his wife Emily Ayers discovered that they were having twins, so they moved back to their hometown of Albany, New York. He works there as an appellate lawyer.

SOURCES FOR EPIGRAPHS

Front: CHUANG TZU, BASIC WRITINGS 37–38 (B. Watson trans. 1964).

Part One: James D. Gordon III, *How Not to Succeed in Law School*, 100 YALE L.J. 1679, 1692 (1991).

1: Paul Savoy, *Toward a New Politics of Legal Education*, 79 YALE L.J. 444, 487 (1970).

2: UNITED STATES AIR FORCE MANUAL 64–3: SURVIVAL TRAINING EDITION 6 (1956).

3: MARK TWAIN, *Journalism in Tennessee*, THE COMPLETE SHORT STORIES OF MARK TWAIN 31 (Charles Neider ed. 1957).

Part Two: Grant Gilmore, *Legal Realism: Its Cause and Cure*, 100 YALE L.J. 1037, 1041 (1961).

4: KARL LLEWELLYN, THE COMMON LAW TRADITION: DECIDING APPEALS 28 (1960).

5: DOUGLAS ADAMS, THE HITCHHIKER'S GUIDE TO THE GALAXY, ch. 28 (1979).

6: STEPHEN VINCENT BENÉT, THE DEVIL AND DANIEL WEBSTER, 14–15 (1937 ed.).

Part Three: HENRY TETLOW, WE FARM FOR A HOBBY—AND MAKE IT PAY 41 (1942).

7: *The Oprah Winfrey Show*, Oct. 18, 1996, quoted in John Young, *Toni Morrison, Oprah Winfrey, and Postmodern Popular Audiences*, AFRICAN-AMERICAN REV., June 22, 2001.

8: PLATO, MENO 79e–80a, trans. W.K.C. Guthrie (COLLECTED DIALOGUES, ed. Edith Hamilton & Huntington Cairns 1961).

9: JOHN DAIDO LOORI, CAVE OF TIGERS: THE LIVING ZEN PRACTICE OF DHARMA COMBAT 162 (2008).

10: CAPT. JOHN W. TRIMMER, HOW TO AVOID HUGE SHIPS 4 (2d ed. 1993).

11: CALVIN C. BISHOP, SLIDE RULE AND HOW TO USE IT vi (1945);
FRIEDRICH NIETZSCHE, BEYOND GOOD AND EVIL 98 (1907).

Part Four: KARL N. LLEWELLYN, THE BRAMBLE BUSH: THE CLASSIC LECTURES
ON THE LAW AND LAW SCHOOL 101 (repr. 2008).

13: SHUNRYU SUZUKI, ZEN MIND, BEGINNER'S MIND: INFORMAL TALKS ON ZEN
MEDITATION AND PRACTICE 21 (1970, repr. 2011).

14: ARISTOTLE, NICOMACHEAN ETHICS 1103a33–35, as translated by W.D. Ross in
INTRODUCTION TO ARISTOTLE 331 (ed. Richard McKeon 1947).

15: SANDRA BEASLEY, "Vocation," in I WAS THE JUKEBOX (2010).

16: Duncan Kennedy, *How Law School Fails: A Polemic*, 1 YALE REV. L. & SOC. ACTION
71, 80 (1970).

Conclusion: THOMAS SHAFFER, FAITH AND THE PROFESSIONS 182 (1987).

NOTES

Introduction

1. Weldon B. Johnson, *Valley Boy, 7, Conquers Alcatraz Waters*, ARIZ. REPUBLIC, May 22, 2006.

2. Kennon M. Sheldon & Lawrence S. Krieger, *Understanding the Negative Effects of Legal Education on Law Students: A Longitudinal Test of Self-Determination Theory*, 33 PERSONALITY & SOC. PSYCHOL. BULL. 883, 883 (2007). *See also* Susan Daicoff, *Lawyer, Be Thyself: An Empirical Investigation of the Relationship Between the Ethic of Care, the Feeling Decisionmaking Preference, and Lawyer Wellbeing*, 16 VA. J. SOC. POL'Y & L. 87, 93–101 (2008) (discussing high levels of depression, alcoholism, and general psychological distress in attorneys and law students).

3. Mitu Gulati, Richard Sander & Robert Sockloskie, *The Happy Charade: An Empirical Examination of the Third Year of Law School*, 51 J. LEGAL EDUC. 235 (2001).

4. ANTHONY T. KRONMAN, THE LOST LAWYER: FAILING IDEALS OF THE LEGAL PROFESSION 134–46 (1993).

5. Brian Tamanaha's book *Failing Law Schools*, published in 2012, argues that law school is a bad bet for many law students. Tamanaha offers startling statistics about law students' prospects of finding jobs after law school, and the debt burden they emerge with. The specific numbers in the book may become dated in the near future, but the concerns Tamanaha raises will still be worth knowing about. Much of the debate on whether law school is economically worthwhile is playing out on blogs and in newspapers, so use Tamanaha as a starting point, but spend some time with Google to catch up with the debate.

6. DUNCAN KENNEDY, LEGAL EDUCATION AND THE REPRODUCTION OF HIERARCHY: A POLEMIC AGAINST THE SYSTEM (repr. 2007).

7. Martha C. Nussbaum, *Cultivating Humanity in Legal Education*, 70 U. CHI. L. REV. 265 (2003).

8. Gary Bellow, *On Talking Tough to Each Other: Comments on Condlin*, 33 J. LEGAL EDUC. 619, 622–23 (1983).

9. OLIVER WENDELL HOLMES, JR., *The Law, in* THE ESSENTIAL HOLMES: SELECTIONS FROM THE LETTERS, SPEECHES, JUDICIAL OPINIONS, AND OTHER WRITINGS OF OLIVER WENDELL HOLMES, JR. 221, 224 (Richard A. Posner ed., 1992).

Part One

1. ROY STUCKEY ET AL., BEST PRACTICES FOR LEGAL EDUCATION: A VISION AND A ROAD MAP 178 (2007).

2. *Id.* at 177.

3. Talbot D'Alemberte, *Talbot D'Alemberte on Legal Education*, 76 A.B.A. J. 52, 52 (Sept. 1990), *quoted in id.* at 177.

Chapter One

1. *Quoted in* Steve Sheppard, *An Informal History of How Law Schools Evaluate Students, with a Predictable Emphasis on Law School Final Exams*, 65 UMKC L. REV. 657, 678 (1997).

2. Lyrissa Lidsky, *Exam Trials and Errors*, posting on Prawfsblawg, http://prawfsblawg .blogs.com (Jan. 4, 2010, 8:07 p.m.).

3. Justin Kruger, Dale T. Miller & Derrick Wirtz, *Counterfactual Thinking and the First-Instinct Fallacy*, 88 J. PERSONALITY & SOC. PSYCHOL. 725 (2005) (which contains a review of studies dating back to 1929).

4. *Id.* at 726.

Chapter Two

1. CHARLES H. WHITEBREAD, THE EIGHT SECRETS OF TOP EXAM PERFORMANCE IN LAW SCHOOL: AN EASY-TO-USE, STEP-BY-STEP PROGRAM FOR ACHIEVING GREAT GRADES!, at 45 (1995).

2. WARD HILL LAMON, RECOLLECTIONS OF ABRAHAM LINCOLN, 1847–1865, at 173 (1911), *quoted in* DORIS KEARNS GOODWIN, TEAM OF RIVALS: THE POLITICAL GENIUS OF ABRAHAM LINCOLN 586 (2005).

3. Gary D. Sherman, Jonathan Haidt & James A. Coan, *Viewing Cute Images Increases Behavioral Carefulness*, 9 EMOTION 282 (2009).

Chapter Four

1. *See* GRANT MORRISON & DAVE MCKEAN, BATMAN: ARKHAM ASYLUM: SERIOUS HOUSE ON SERIOUS EARTH (1997).

2. DAVID H. BARLOW, CLINICAL HANDBOOK OF PSYCHOLOGICAL DISORDERS: A STEP-BY-STEP TREATMENT MANUAL 474 (4th ed. 2007).

3. Ilott v. Wilkes, 106 Eng. Rep. 674 (K.B. 1820).

4. 18 U.S.C. § 2423(b).

5. Exec. Order No. 13,292 § 4.1(a)(3), 68 Fed. Reg. 15,315, 15,332 (Mar. 25, 2003).

6. Tuohey v. Trans Nat'l. Travel Inc., 47 Pa. D. & C. 3d 250 (1987).

7. U.S. CONST. amend. V.

8. Kentucky v. Whorton, 441 U.S. 786, 789 (1979) (emphasis added).

9. For an enlightening discussion of the uses of factor-propositions, *see* CASS R. SUNSTEIN, LEGAL REASONING AND POLITICAL CONFLICT 28–30 (1996).

10. 274 U.S. 200 (1927).

11. See Paul Lombardo's gripping article *Three Generations, No Imbeciles: New Light on Buck v. Bell*, 60 N.Y.U. L. REV. 30 (1985).

12. *See* H.L.A. HART, THE CONCEPT OF LAW 79–99 (2d ed. 1994).

13. *See, e.g.*, Robert M. Cover, *Nomos and Narrative*, 97 HARV. L. REV. 4 (1983) ("No set of legal institutions or prescriptions exists apart from the narratives that locate it and give it meaning.").

14. RONALD DWORKIN, LAW'S EMPIRE 256 (1986).

15. ANTONIN SCALIA, A MATTER OF INTERPRETATION 23 (1997).

16. Frank Easterbrook, *The Court and the Economic System*, 98 HARV. L. REV. 4, 14 (1984).

17. *See* FRIEDRICH KESSLER, GRANT GILMORE & ANTHONY T. KRONMAN, CONTRACTS: CASES AND MATERIALS 553–64 (3d ed. 1986).

18. 85 HARV. L. REV. 1089, 1089 n.2 (1972) (citing Harry Wellington).

19. Marbury v. Madison, 5 U.S. (1 Cranch) 137 (1803).

20. KARL N. LLEWELLYN, THE COMMON LAW TRADITION: DECIDING APPEALS 201 (1960).

21. ANTHONY T. KRONMAN, THE LOST LAWYER: FAILING IDEALS OF THE LEGAL PROFESSION 134–46 (1993).

22. *Id.* at 140.

Chapter Five

1. 539 U.S. 558 (2003).

2. TEXAS CONST. art. 1 § 32(b).

3. *See* Dave Montgomery, *Texas' Gay Marriage Ban May Have Banned All Marriages*, FORTH WORTH STAR-TELEGRAM, Nov. 18, 2009.

4. Lawrence, 539 U.S. at 590 (Scalia, J., dissenting).

5. MODEL PENAL CODE § 4.01(1).

6. M'Naghten's Case, 8 Eng. Rep. 718 (1843).

7. AUSTIN GROSSMAN, SOON I WILL BE INVINCIBLE 5, 8 (2007).

8. *Id.* AT 44.

9. *Id.* at 83, 75.

10. ANTONIN SCALIA & BRYAN A. GARNER, MAKING YOUR CASE: THE ART OF PERSUADING JUDGES 83 (2008). The lawyer's identity has apparently been lost to history.

11. *See* United States v. Carroll Towing Co., 159 F.2d 169 (2d Cir. 1947).

12. N.J. STAT. ANN. § 2C:39.3(k) (emphasis added); *see* Eugene Volokh, *Use Those*

Handcuffs for Manifestly Appropriate Purposes Only, Please, The Volokh Conspiracy (Mar. 3, 2009, 2:31 p.m.), http://www.volokh.com/posts/1236108667.shtml.

13. *See* Maryland v. Shatzer, 130 S. Ct. 1213 (2010).

Chapter Six

1. Travis Proulx & Steven J. Heine, *Connections from Kafka: Exposure to Meaning Threats Improves Implicit Learning of an Artificial Grammar,* 20 PSYCHOL. SCI. 1125 (2009).

2. RICHARD A. POSNER, PROBLEMS OF JURISPRUDENCE 104 (1990).

3. ANTONIN SCALIA, A MATTER OF INTERPRETATION: FEDERAL COURTS AND THE LAW 31–32 (1997).

4. Michael Kent Curtis & Shannon Gilreath, *Transforming Teenagers into Oral Sex Felons: The Persistence of the Crime Against Nature After* Lawrence v. Texas, 43 WAKE FOREST L. REV. 155, 213 n.313 & 314 and accompanying text (2008). For debate on *Brown* and the intent of the framers, *see* Michael J. Klarman, *Brown, Originalism and Constitutional Theory: A Response to Professor McConnell,* 81 VA. L. REV. 1881 (1995).

5. So named for the case that established it, Murray v. The Charming Betsy, 6 U.S. (2 Cranch) 64 (1804).

6. Karl N. Llewellyn, *Remarks on the Theory of Appellate Decision and the Rules or Canons About How Statutes Are to Be Construed,* 3 VAND. L. REV. 395, 401 (1950).

7. Justice Scalia, for example, thinks Llewellyn was being too cute. SCALIA, *supra* note 3, at 26–27.

8. KARL N. LLEWELLYN, THE COMMON LAW TRADITION: DECIDING APPEALS 77–91 (1960).

9. FREDERICK F. SCHAUER, THINKING LIKE A LAWYER: A NEW INTRODUCTION TO LEGAL REASONING 56–57 (2009).

10. *See, e.g.,* LLOYD WEINREB, LEGAL REASON: THE USE OF ANALOGY IN LEGAL ARGUMENT 4 (2005).

11. As observed by many commentators. *See* Thomas B. Marvell & Carlisle E. Moody, *The Lethal Effects of Three-Strikes Laws,* 30 J. LEGAL STUD. 89, 91–92 (2001).

12. The possibility of greater police interest is pointed out in Steven Shavell, *A Note on Marginal Deterrence,* 12 INT'L REV. L. & ECON. 345 (1992), *cited in id.* at 92 n.17.

13. Caleb Mason, *Jay-Z's 99 Problems: A Close Reading with Fourth Amendment Guidance for Cops and Perps* (forthcoming, available at http://slu.edu/Documents/law /Law%20Journal/Archives/LJ56-2_Mason_Article.pdf).

14. 509 U.S. 579 (1993).

15. Daubert v. Merrell Dow Pharmaceuticals, Inc., 43 F.3d 1311, 1316 (9th Cir. 1995).

16. *See* Mark Spottswood, *Live Hearings and Paper Trials,* 38 FLA. ST. U. L. REV. 827 (2011).

17. New York State Bd. of Elections v. Lopez Torres, 552 U.S. 196, 801 (2008) (Stevens, J., concurring) (quoting Thurgood Marshall) .

18. 52 N.Y.2d 542 (1981).

19. *See* Michael Herz, *"Do Justice!": Variations of a Thrice-Told Tale,* 82 VA. L. REV. 111 (1996). Holmes also said, on other occasions, "I hate justice." *See id.*

20. Holmes, *The Path of the Law,* 10 HARV. L. REV. 457 (1897), *reprinted in* THE ESSENTIAL

HOLMES: SELECTIONS FROM THE LETTERS, SPEECHES, JUDICIAL OPINIONS, AND OTHER WRITINGS OF OLIVER WENDELL HOLMES, JR. 160, 176 (Richard A. Posner ed., 1992).

21. WILLIAM BLACKSTONE, 2 COMMENTARIES ON THE LAW OF ENGLAND 2596 (ed. William Carey Jones 1916). People do disagree about what the ratio ought to be. *See* Alexander Volokh, *"n Guilty Men,"* 146 U. PA. L. REV. 173 (1997).

22. MARC GALANTER, LOWERING THE BAR: LAWYER JOKES & LEGAL CULTURE 51 (2005), quoting Thomas Reed Powell.

23. 548 F.2d 415 (2d Cir. 1976).

24. The judge was Lord Bowen, in Edgington v. Fitzmaurice (1882), L.R. 29 Ch.Div. 459, 483, quoted in lots of law review articles, including Curtis Bridgeman & Karen Sandrik, *Bullshit Promises*, 76 TENN. L. REV. 379, 383 (2009).

25. POSNER, *supra* note 2, at 46.

26. Board of Ed. of Independent School Dist. No. 92 of Pottawatomie County v. Earls, 536 U.S. 822 (2002).

27. *Id.* at 851–52.

28. *Id.* at 852.

29. HOLMES, *The Activity of Law, in* THE ESSENTIAL HOLMES, *supra* note 20, at 171. Judge Posner says we now know it does. POSNER, THE PROBLEMATICS OF MORAL AND LEGAL THEORY 212 (1999).

30. Clinton v. Jones, 520 U.S. 681, 702 (1997).

31. DAVID LUBAN, LAWYERS AND JUSTICE: AN ETHICAL STUDY 69 (1988).

32. Daniel Markovits, *Legal Ethics from the Lawyer's Point of View*, 15 YALE J.L. & HUMAN. 209, 218 (2003).

33. MARTHA C. NUSSBAUM, CULTIVATING HUMANITY: A CLASSICAL DEFENSE OF REFORM IN LIBERAL EDUCATION 10–11 (1997).

34. JOHNNIE COCHRAN, A LAWYER'S LIFE 11 (2002).

35. WALTER FISHER, WHAT EVERY LAWYER KNOWS 89 (1974).

36. JAMES BOYD WHITE, THE LEGAL IMAGINATION 210 (abridged ed. 1985).

Chapter Seven

1. BRYAN A. GARNER, THE ELEMENTS OF LEGAL STYLE 2 (2d ed. 2002).

2. Rylands v. Fletcher, L.R. 3 H.L. 330 (1868).

3. Marbury v. Madison, 5 U.S. (1 Cranch) 137 (1803).

Chapter Eight

1. Phillip E. Areeda, *The Socratic Method (SM) (Lecture at Puget Sound, 1/31/90)*, 109 HARV. L. REV. 911, 919 (1996).

2. ELIZABETH MERTZ, THE LANGUAGE OF LAW SCHOOL: LEARNING TO "THINK LIKE A LAWYER" 141, 144 (2007); Orin S. Kerr, *The Decline of the Socratic Method at Harvard*, 78 NEB. L. REV. 113 (1999).

3. MERTZ, *supra* note 2, at 200.

4. Elizabeth Garrett, *Becoming Lawyers: The Role of the Socratic Method in Modern Law Schools*, 1 GREEN BAG 2D 199, 201 (1998) (book review).
5. I am grateful to David A. Finkelstein for this observation.
6. Areeda, *supra* note 1, at 918.
7. SUSAN ESTRICH, HOW TO GET INTO LAW SCHOOL 175 (2004).
8. SHANA CONNELL NOYES & HENRY S. NOYES, ACING YOUR FIRST YEAR OF LAW SCHOOL: THE TEN STEPS TO SUCCESS YOU WON'T LEARN FROM Class 27 (2d ed. 2008).
9. Areeda, *supra* note 1, at 918.
10. *See, e.g.*, Michael Vitiello, *Professor Kingsfield: The Most Misunderstood Character in Literature*, 33 HOFSTRA L. REV. 955 (2005).
11. Scott H. Greenfield, *The Slackoisie Go to Law School*, Simple Justice: A New York Criminal Defense Blog (August 23, 2008, 5:05 a.m.), http://blog.simplejustice .us/2008/08/23/the-slackoisie-go-to-law-school.aspx; *see also* Scott H. Greenfield, *In Defense of the Socratic Method*, Simple Justice: A New York Criminal Defense Blog (May 11, 2009, 6:29 a.m.), http://blog.simplejustice.us/2009/05/11/in-defense-of -the-socratic-method.aspx.
12. KARL N. LLEWELLYN, THE COMMON LAW TRADITION: DECIDING APPEALS 355 (1960).

Chapter Nine

1. The "two-classes-in-a-row-rule" is apparently established wisdom at many law schools, although it wasn't at mine. I'm grateful to David A. Finkelstein for letting me know about it.
2. KARL N. LLEWELLYN, THE BRAMBLE BUSH: THE CLASSIC LECTURES ON THE LAW AND LAW SCHOOL 153 (repr. 2008).
3. *Id.* at 102.

Chapter Ten

1. The cases cited were assigned in Neal Katyal's criminal law class at Georgetown, and were included in a draft of the casebook *Criminal Law* by Professor Katyal, Tracey Meares, and Dan Kahan. The cases are People v. Newton, 8 Cal. App. 3d 359, 87 Cal. Rptr. 394 (1970); State v. Jerrett, 309 N.C. 239, 307 S.E.2d 339 (1983); and Baird v. State, 604 N.E. 2d 1170 (Ind. 1992).
2. Prey v. Kruse, No. 08 Civ. 287, 2009 WL 425031, at *6 (S.D. Ohio Feb. 19, 2009).
3. Woods-Leber v. Hyatt Hotels of P.R., 124 F.3d 47, 52 (1st Cir. 1997).
4. The article referred to is Paul Butler, *Racially Based Jury Nullification: Black Power in the Criminal Justice System*, 105 YALE L.J. 677 (1995). "Jury nullification" is when a jury believes the defendant committed the crime, but refuses to convict anyway, "nullifying" the law in question.
5. VLADIMIR NABOKOV, LECTURES ON LITERATURE 3 (2002).
6. David Cole, *Laptops vs. Learning*, WASH. POST, Apr. 7, 2007, at A13.

7.　Kevin Yamamoto, *Banning Laptops in the Classroom: Is It Worth the Hassle?*, 57 J. Legal Educ. 477 (2007).

Chapter Eleven

1.　D. Moshman & M. Geil, *Collaborative Reasoning: Evidence for Collective Rationality*, in 4 Thinking and Reasoning 231 (1998).

2.　Shana Connell Noyes & Henry S. Noyes, Acing Your First Year of Law School: The Ten Steps to Success You Won't Learn in Class 34 (1999).

Chapter Twelve

1.　*See* A. Benjamin Spencer, *The Law School Critique in Historical Perspective*, Wash. & Lee. L. Rev (forthcoming).

2.　William M. Sullivan, Anne Colby, Judith Welch Wegner, Lloyd Bond & Lee S. Shulman, Educating Lawyers: Preparation for the Profession of Law (2007).

3.　You can read more about these efforts to expand the law school curriculum at the website of Educating Tomorrow's Lawyers, a consortium of law schools led by the primary author of the Carnegie Report. *See* http://educatingtomorrowslawyers .du.edu.

4.　Yale Law School, Clinics and Experiential Learning, http://www.law.yale.edu/ academics/clinicalopportunities.htm (visited Sept. 2, 2012).

5.　*See* Sullivan et al., *supra* note 2, at 100–101 (discussing professors' negative attitudes toward clinics).

6.　Gary L. Blasi, *What Lawyers Know: Lawyering Expertise, Cognitive Science, and the Functions of Theory*, 45 J. Legal Educ. 313, 359 (1995).

7.　*Id.*

8.　There is an interesting discussion of how students' views on the death penalty were affected by experiences in a clinic representing death-row inmates in David Luban & Michael Millemann, *Good Judgment: Ethics Teaching in Dark Times*, 9 Geo. J. Legal Ethics 31, 84 (1995). Changes in views were common in the clinic, but of the students who took an affiliated class on death-penalty law, without any clinical component, not a single one changed their views. *Id.*

9.　Todd S. Rakoff & Martha Minow, *A Case for Another Case Method*, 60 Vand. L. Rev. 597 (2007).

10.　Recent efforts to make the problem method part of the core curriculum at Harvard are discussed in *id.*

Part Four

1.　Jerome Frank, in Frank, Pound & Vanderbilt, *What Constitutes a Good Legal Education*, 7 Am. L. Sch. Rev. 887, 900 (1933).

2.　William M. Sullivan, Anne Colby, Judith Welch Wegner, Lloyd Bond & Lee

S. SHULMAN, EDUCATING LAWYERS: PREPARATION FOR THE PROFESSION OF LAW 76 (2007).

3.   Savoy, *Toward a New Politics of Legal Education*, 79 YALE L.J. 444, 446.

Chapter Thirteen

1.   *See* TAO LE &VIKAS BHUSHAN, FIRST AID FOR THE WARDS 166–67 (3d ed. 2005). The acronym stands for Serositis, Oral ulcers, Arthritis, Photosensitivity, Blood abnormalities, Renal disorder, Antinuclear antibody test positive, Immunologic disorder, Neurologic disorder, Malar rash, and Discoid rash.

2.   Gary L. Blasi, *What Lawyers Know: Lawyering Expertise, Cognitive Science, and the Functions of Theory*, 45 J. LEGAL EDUC. 313, 338 (1995).

3.   Daniel Kahneman & Gary Klein, *Conditions for Intuitive Expertise: A Failure to Disagree*, 64 AM. PSYCHOLOGIST 515 (2009).

4.   Gary Klein et al., *Rapid Decision Making on the Fireground*, in 1 PROCEEDINGS OF THE HUMAN FACTORS AND ERGONOMICS SOC. 30TH ANN. MTG. 576 (1986), cited in Kahneman & Klein, *supra* note 3.

5.   Goodman-Delahunty et al., *Insightful or Wishful: Lawyers' Ability to Predict Case Outcomes*, 16 PSYCHOL. PUB. POL'Y & L. 133, 144 (2010).

6.   DONALD A. SCHÖN, THE REFLECTIVE PRACTITIONER: HOW PROFESSIONALS THINK IN ACTION 61 (1984).

7.   Blasi, *supra* note 2, at 323.

8.   DAVID FREDERICK, SUPREME COURT AND APPELLATE ADVOCACY 289 (2003).

9.   *Id.*, quoting Glockman v. Wileman Bros. & Elliott, Inc., No. 95-1184, 1996 WL 700569 at 29–32 (Dec. 2, 1996).

10.   *Id.* at 220.

11.   Chen-Bo Zhong et al., *Good Lamps Are the Best Police: Darkness Increases Dishonesty and Self-Interested Behavior*, 21 PSYCHOL. SCIENCE 311 (2010).

12.   Katie Liljenquist et al., *The Smell of Virtue: Clean Scents Promote Reciprocity and Charity*, 21 PSYCHOL. SCIENCE 381 (2010). The study was not funded by Windex.

13.   Simone Schnall et al., *Disgust as Embodied Moral Judgment*, 34 PERSONALITY & SOC. PSYCHOL. BULL. 1096 (2008).

14.   Shai Danzigera, Jonathan Levavb & Liora Avnaim-Pessoa, *Extraneous factors in judicial decisions*, 108 PNAS 6889 (April 26, 2011).

15.   Studies of various biases have found that awareness of psychological bias allows people to predict other people's behavior better—but it doesn't help them de-bias their own behavior. *See, e.g.*, Jane Goodman Delahunty et al., *Insightful or Wishful: Lawyers' Ability to Predict Case Outcomes*, 16 PSYCHOL. PUB. POL'Y & L. 133 (2010); *see also* Timothy D. Wilson et al., *Mental Contamination and the Debiasing Problem*, in HEURISTICS AND BIASES 185 (Thomas Gilovich et al. ed., 2002).

16.   Emily Pronin et al., *The Bias Blind Spot: Perceptions of Bias in Self Versus Others*, 28 PERSONALITY & SOC. PSYCHOL. BULL. 369 (2002).

17.   Rebecca Sandefur & Jeffrey Selbin, *The Clinic Effect*, 16 CLINICAL L. REV. 57, 78

(2009) (reviewing studies; if you want to understand why clinical legal education exists, this article is a nice place to start); *see* Richard J. Wilson, *Western Europe: Last Holdout in the Worldwide Acceptance of Clinical Legal Education*, 10 GERMAN L.J. 823, 826 (2009) (counting about eight hundred law school clinics in the United States).

18. Sandefur & Selbin, *supra* note 17, at 85–86.
19. Summers v. Tice, 199 P.2d 1 (Cal. 1948).

Chapter Fourteen

1. RICHARD A. POSNER, LAW AND LITERATURE 339 (3d ed. 2009).
2. Richard A. Posner, *Goodbye to the Bluebook*, 53 U. CHI. L. REV. 1343, 1350 (1986).
3. *Id.*
4. One of the most influential is DAVID A. BINDER ET AL., LAWYERS AS COUNSELORS: A CLIENT-CENTERED APPROACH (2d ed. 2004).
5. *See* Garth & Martin, *Law Schools and the Construction of Competence*, 43 J. LEGAL EDUC. 469 (1993).
6. Jerome Frank, *A Plea for Lawyer-Schools*, 56 YALE L.J. 1303, 1306 (1947).

Chapter Fifteen

1. The estimate of how many hours per week it takes to reach 1,900 billable hours per year is Deborah Rhode's. *See* DEBORAH L. RHODE, IN THE INTERESTS OF JUSTICE: REFORMING THE LEGAL PROFESSION 10 (2003).
2. *Quoted in id.* at 170.
3. American Bar Association, *Average Amount Borrowed for Law School*, at www.abanet .org/legaled/statistics/charts/stats—20.pdf. (I rounded to the nearest thousand.)
4. Several reports have suggested that debt deters students from entering public interest. But Christa McGill argues that debt does not deter public interest work, in *Educational Debt and Law Student Failure to Enter Public Service Careers: Bringing Empirical Data to Bear*, 31 LAW & SOC. INQUIRY 677 (2006).
5. Philip G. Schrag, *Why Would Anyone Want to Be a Public Interest Lawyer?* (Sept. 23, 2009), available at http://papers.ssrn.com/s013/papers.cfm?abstract_id=1486246.
6. Testimony of John Roberts, Sept. 15, 2005 (response to question from Sen. Durbin).
7. *Id.* at 133.

Chapter Sixteen

1. Two excellent books on legal ethics—which take very different positions on how lawyers should conduct themselves—are David Luban's *Lawyers and Justice* (1988) and W. Bradley Wendel's *Lawyers and Fidelity to Law* (2010).
2. Linda Ross Meyer, *Is Practical Reason Mindless?*, 86 GEO. L.J. 647, 657 (1998).

3. Susan Daicoff, *Lawyer, Be Thyself: An Empirical Investigation of the Relationship Between the Ethic of Care, the Feeling Decisionmaking Preference, and Lawyer Wellbeing*, 16 VA. J. SOC. POL'Y & L. 87, 95–96 (2008).

4. *See* ELIZABETH MERTZ, THE LANGUAGE OF LAW SCHOOL: LEARNING TO "THINK LIKE A LAWYER" 185–90 (2007).

5. The research is summarized in *id*.

6. Suzanne Homer & Lois Schwartz, *Admitted but Not Accepted: Outsiders Take an Inside Look at Law School*, 5 BERKELEY WOMEN'S L.J. 1, 33 (1990).

7. *See* MERTZ, *supra* note 4, at 186–90.

8. LANI GUINIER ET AL., BECOMING GENTLEMEN: WOMEN, LAW SCHOOL, AND INSTITUTIONAL CHANGE (1997).

9. MERTZ, *supra* note 4, at 174, 179.

10. Bonita London et al., *Studying Institutional Engagement*, 30 HARV. J.L. & GENDER 389 (2007).

11. *Note, Making Docile Lawyers: An Essay on the Pacification of Law Students*, 111 Harv. L. Rev. 2027 (1998). This Note was authored by Sharon Dolovich. The phrase "total institutions" is from ERVING GOFFMAN, ASYLUMS: ESSAYS ON THE CONDITION OF THE SOCIAL SITUATION OF MENTAL PATIENTS AND OTHER INMATES (1951).

12. M. Todd Henderson, *Citing Fiction*, 11 GREEN BAG 2D 171, 185 (2008).

13. *See* John Valenti & Jennifer Sinco Kelleher, *Judge Voids Mortgage*, NEWSDAY, Nov. 25, 2009.

14. LINCOLN CAPLAN, SKADDEN: POWER, MONEY, AND THE RISE OF A LEGAL EMPIRE 147 (1993).

15. Jeffrey M. Jones, *Automobile, Banking Industry Images Slide Further*, Gallup.com, Jan. 21, 2010. Lawyers' positive ratings are at 25 percent for 2009.

16. Judson Mills, *Changes in Moral Attitudes Following Temptation*, 26 J. PERSONALITY 517, 528 (1958).

17. *Id*. at 529.

18. For an entertaining introduction to cognitive dissonance, try chapter 1 of CAROL TAVRIS & ELLIOTT ARONSON, MISTAKES WERE MADE (BUT NOT BY ME) (2007).

19. Mills, *supra* note 16, at 531.

20. *See* TAVRIS & ARONSON, *supra* note 18, at 38–39; ROBERT B. CIALDINI, INFLUENCE: THE PSYCHOLOGY OF PERSUASION 103–111 (rev. ed. 2007).

21. ANTHONY T. KRONMAN, THE LOST LAWYER: FAILING IDEALS OF THE LEGAL PROFESSION 66–71 (1993).

22. DAVID LUBAN, LEGAL ETHICS AND HUMAN DIGNITY 295 (2007).

Conclusion

1. According to Javier Grillo-Marxuach, writer for *Lost* and the sadly underrated show *The Middleman* on ABC Family, as quoted in ANDY BOYNTON, WILL FISCHER & WILLIAM BOLE, THE IDEA HUNTER: HOW TO FIND THE BEST IDEAS AND MAKE THEM HAPPEN 135 (2011).

2. *See* Lawrence T. Frase & Barry J. Schwartz, *Effect of Question Production and Answering on Prose Recall*, 67 J. EDUC. PSYCHOL. 628 (1975).

3. DAVID LUBAN, LEGAL ETHICS AND HUMAN DIGNITY 297 (2007).

4. CARLA NEEDLEMAN, THE WORK OF CRAFT 17 (1979).

5. *Id.* at 137.

6. *Id.*

7. Elena Kagan, *Richard Posner: The Judge*, 120 HARV. L. REV. 1121 (2007).

INDEX